Adobe Illustrator CC
Graphic Design & Custom Illustrations

Illustrator is a graphic design tool used to allow the creation of custom illustrations for use in artwork. A similar program, such as **Photoshop**, is primarily used to adjust photos. However, **Illustrator** will open your creative side to develop logos, and symbols, create artwork and allow unique warping of text to create unusual effects. Artistic and 3D effects are commonly used to give your artwork a different look. This program will create vector graphics which are the mathematical definitions of lines, boxes, and circles. It will also teach important skills such as how to use selection techniques, **Text Tools**, **Drawing Tools**, and advanced formatting techniques. We are only offering the fundamentals manual at this time. Once you understand the style of the program, you will be able to continue the learning process on your own. The features covered are very similar to **Illustrator CS4**, **CS5**, **CS6**, and **Mac CS6** commands.

Table of Contents

<u>Copyright and Release Information</u>

This workbook/guide was updated on **3/17/2023** and redesigned for **Adobe Illustrator CC**. This guide is the sole property of **Jeff Hutchinson** and **eLearnLogic.** Any emailing, copying, duplication, or reproduction of this guide, must be approved by **Jeff Hutchinson** in writing. However, students who take a class or purchase the guide are free to use it for personal development and learning.

ISBN-13: 978-1987724035   ISBN-10: 1987724038

Exercise Download

Exercises are posted on the website and can be downloaded to your computer.
Please do the following:

Open Internet Explorer/Edge:    Or Google Chrome:

Type the web address:

elearnlogic.com/download/illustratorcc-1.exe

You might get several security warnings, but answer yes and run through each one. When you click
"Unzip," the files will be located in **C:\Data\IllustratorCC-1** folder.

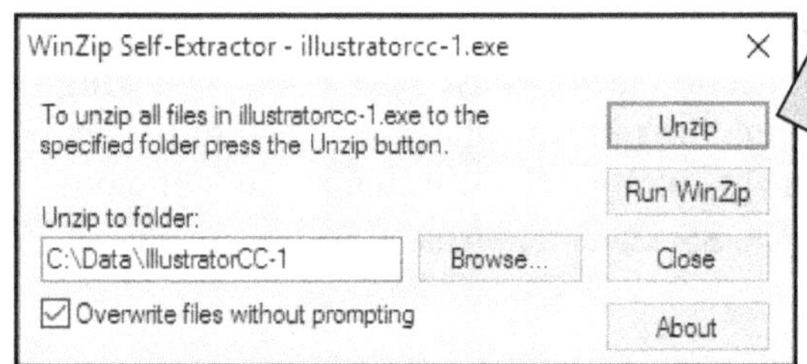

If there are any questions or problems, please contact Jeff Hutchinson at:

JeffHutch@elearnlogic.com

Note: For Mac users, download the file at:
elearnlogic.com/download/illustratorcc-1.zip

About the Author

Jeff Hutchinson is a computer instructor teaching a variety of classes around the country. He has a BS
degree from BYU in Computer-Aided Engineering and has worked in the Information Technology field
supporting and maintaining computers for many years. He also previously owned a computer training and
consulting firm in San Francisco, California. After selling his business in 2001, he has continued to work
as an independent computer instructor/consultant around the country. **Jeff Hutchinson** currently lives in
Utah and also provides training for the Utah Valley University Community Education system, offering
valuable computer skills for the general knowledge of students, career development, and career
advancement. Understanding the technology and the needs of students has been the basis for developing
this material. **Jeff Hutchinson** can be contacted at jeffhutch@elearnlogic.com or **(801) 376-6687**.

Design Strategy

This workbook is designed in conjunction with an **Online-Instructor-Led course** (for more information
see: **www.elearnlogic.com**). Unlike other computer guides, students will not need to review lengthy
procedures in order to understand a topic. All that is necessary are the brief statements and command
paths located within the guide that demonstrate how a concept is used. There are many **Step-By-Step
Practice Exercises** and more comprehensive **Student Projects** offered to help students better understand
concepts. Furthermore, they will find that this workbook/guide can often be used as a reference to help
them understand concepts quickly and thoroughly. An index is also provided on the last page to reference
important topics as necessary. However, if more detail is needed for study, the Internet can be used, as
well, to search for a concept. Also, if students' skills are weak due to lack of use, you can refresh your
knowledge quickly by visually scanning the numbered concepts to test them out.

Manual Organization

The following are special formatting conventions:

- **Numbered Sections** on the left are the **Concepts** covered.
- **Bold Italic Text** is used to highlight commands that will perform the **Concept** or procedure in
  completing the practice exercises.
- **Practice Exercises** are a **Step-by-Step** approach to demonstrating the **Concept.**
- **Student Projects** are a more comprehensive approach to demonstrating the **Concept.**
- **Dark, Grayed-Out Sections** are optional/advanced **Concepts.**
- **Bolded** items are important **Concepts,** terminology, or commands used.
- **Tip** - These are additional ideas about the **Concept.**

Chapter 1 - Interface and Menu Overview

If you are new to **Illustrator**, you will need to familiarize yourself with the basic features of the program. First, we will look at the interface and the basic navigation features to allow you to get around the program. This interface is different from other applications, and understanding its layout and components is vital to using the program effectively.

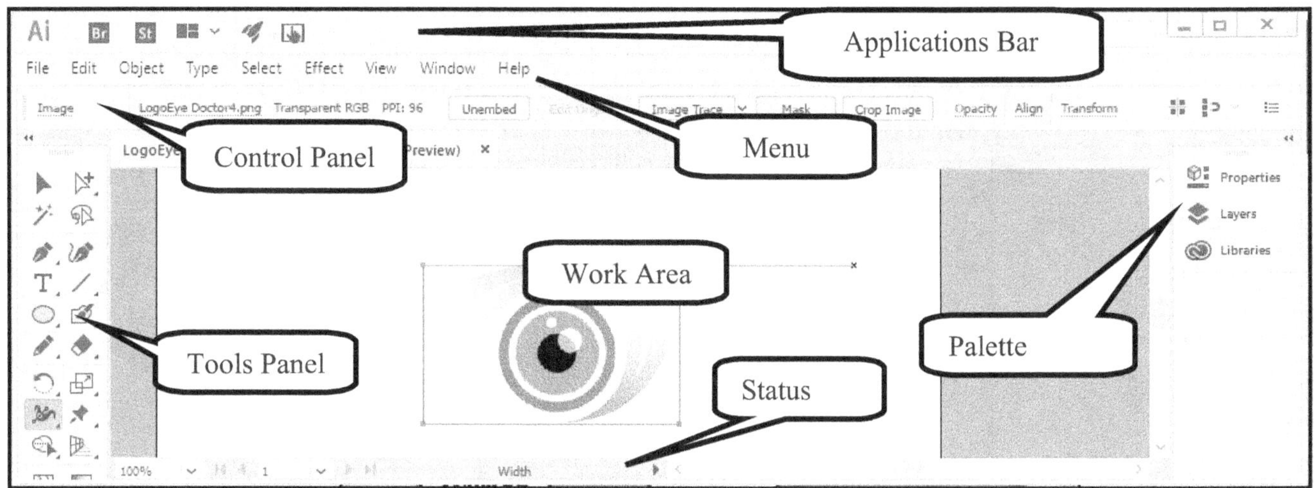

Section 1 – Core Topics

Concept	Explanation / *Command String in italic*
1.1 Exercises	The exercise files on a **PC** are located in **C:\Data\IllustratorCC-1** folder and the **Mac** files are usually stored on the desktop in the **IllustratorCC-1** folder.
Practice Exercise 1 Open File	***File Menu→Open→Navigating the User Interface.ai.***
1.2 Mac Keyboard Commands	There are a few fundamental differences to identify: **Ctrl Key** (Windows) = **Command Key** (Mac). **Alt Key** (Windows) = **Option Key** (Mac). ***Edit Menu→Preferences (Windows)* = *Illustrator Menu→Preferences (Mac).***
1.3 Adobe Terminology	**Industry Term = Adobe Term** **Industry Term = Adobe Term** **Text = Type** **Special Characters = Glyphs** **Border = Stroke** **Transparency = Opacity** **Insert = Place** **Color Samples = Swatches**
1.4 New Document	This will start a new document. ***File Menu→New→*** Letter 612 x 792 pt → Create ***or* Ctrl N *keys.*** Letter 612 x 792 pt Postcard 288 x 560 pt Common 1366 x 768 px iPhone X 1125 x 2436 px HDV/HDTV 1080 1920 x 1080 px More Presets
Practice Exercise 2 New Document	Create a new document: ***File Menu→New→*** Letter 612 x 792 pt .

1.5 Tools Panel	The **Tools Panel** is located on the left side of the screen and contains tools to manipulate pictures. **Tools Group -** This is a small arrow in the lower right corner of the **Tools** icon. By holding the left mouse button on the **Tools** icon, the **Tools Group** will be displayed. **Expand/Collapse Tools** - On top of the **Panel** is a small double arrow. This will expand and collapse all tools into a single column or two columns. Expanded: Collapsed:
1.6 Vector Graphics	These are made up of mathematical equations composed of lines, arcs, circles, and geometric shapes. When you **Select** a segment of an object, the entire object will be **Selected**. Several popular **Vector-based** systems include **Adobe Illustrator**, **Adobe InDesign**, and **Microsoft Visio**. **Tip:** The **Type Tool** creates a new **Vector** layer and can be modified when a Layer is selected. In contrast, a **Raster** layer cannot be modified.
1.7 Raster Graphics	This is an array of small squares called pixels that require more memory and disk space to store. When reducing the resolution of the **Raster** images, there could be a loss in image quality because pixels are eliminated. Example: **Photoshop** and **Paintbrush** are **Raster**-based programs.

1.8 New Artboard	This creates a new **Artboard** space. *CC: File Menu → New →Print Tab →More* *Settings (located in the lower right corner).* *CS6: File Menu →New.* 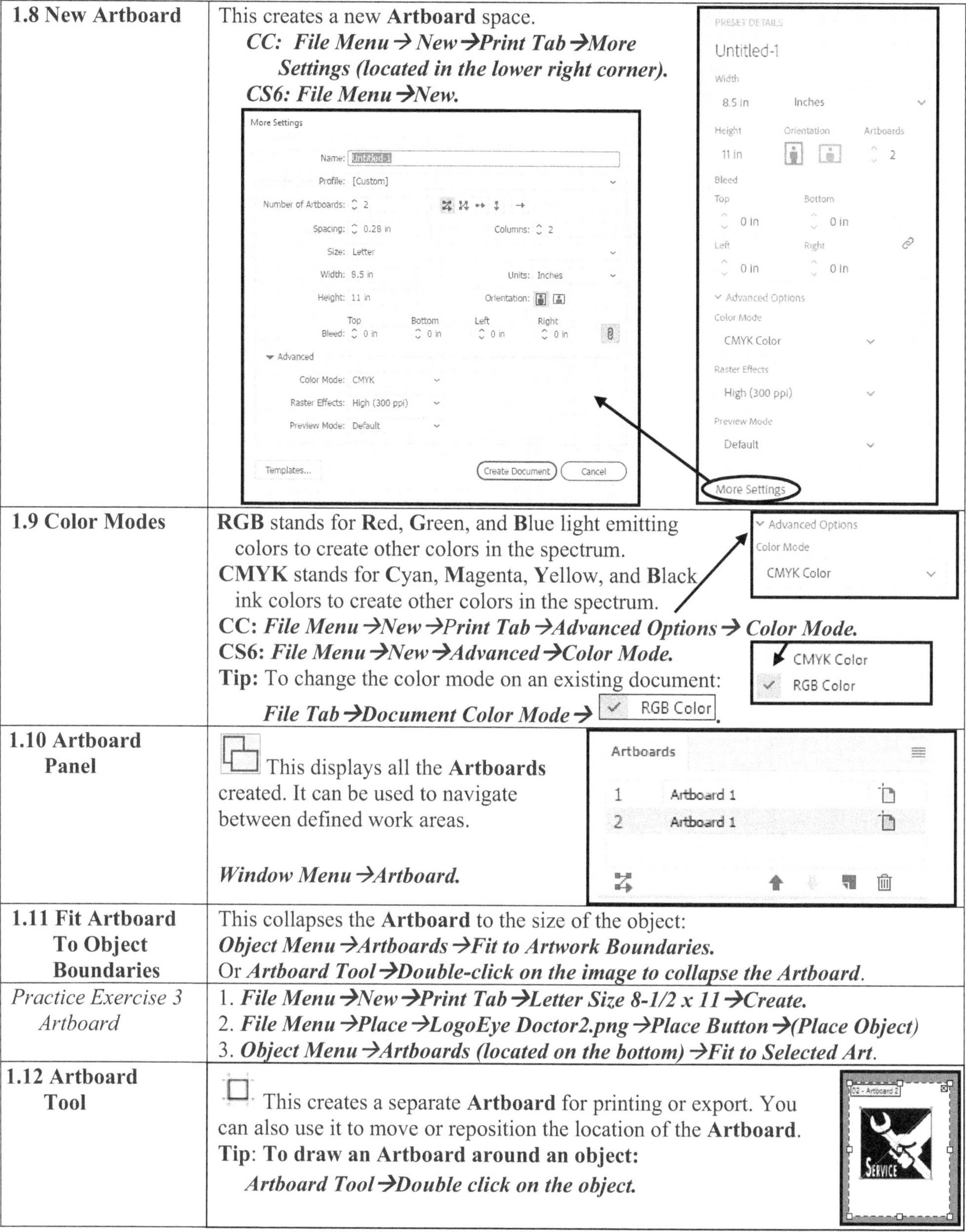

1.9 Color Modes	**RGB** stands for **R**ed, **G**reen, and **B**lue light emitting
	    colors to create other colors in the spectrum.
	CMYK stands for **C**yan, **M**agenta, **Y**ellow, and **B**lack
	    ink colors to create other colors in the spectrum.
	CC: *File Menu →New →Print Tab →Advanced Options → Color Mode.*
	CS6: *File Menu →New →Advanced →Color Mode.*
	Tip: To change the color mode on an existing document:
	    File Tab →Document Color Mode → RGB Color .

1.10 Artboard **Panel**	This displays all the **Artboards** created. It can be used to navigate between defined work areas. *Window Menu →Artboard.*

1.11 Fit Artboard
    To Object
    Boundaries
	This collapses the **Artboard** to the size of the object:
	Object Menu →Artboards →Fit to Artwork Boundaries.
	Or *Artboard Tool →Double-click on the image to collapse the Artboard.*

Practice Exercise 3 *Artboard*	1. *File Menu →New →Print Tab →Letter Size 8-1/2 x 11 →Create.* 2. *File Menu →Place →LogoEye Doctor2.png →Place Button →(Place Object)* 3. *Object Menu →Artboards (located on the bottom) →Fit to Selected Art.*

1.12 Artboard
    Tool
	This creates a separate **Artboard** for printing or export. You can also use it to move or reposition the location of the **Artboard**.
	Tip: To draw an Artboard around an object:
	    Artboard Tool →Double click on the object.

Practice Exercise 4
Artboard Area
	1. *Select the Artboard Tool→Draw a new Artboard area.*
	2. *File Menu→Place→LogoConstruction1.png.*
	3. *Move the image to the New Artboard→*
	   Size the Artboard manually to the desired size.
	4. *File Menu→Export→Save for Web→JPEG - High→*
	   Save Button→File name: Construction.jpg.

Practice Exercise 5 *Place Artboard*	1. *File Menu→New→Print Tab→Size: Letter→Create.* 2. *File Menu→Place→Still Life Apples.jpg (Place in Artboard).* 3. *Artboard Tool→Double Click on the image→Select Artboard in the Artboard Panel.* 4. *File Menu→Export→Export As→Save as Type: JPEG→* *Filename: Test.jpg→Export button→Ok.*
1.13 Hand Tool	This moves **Illustrator Artboards** within the **Illustration Window**. The **Hand Tool** can also be used as a neutral tool to stop action when in the middle of using a command. For example, draw a line using the *Pencil Tool→Press the Hand* to stop drawing. **Tip:** Use the **Artboard Tool** to move a single **Artboard**.

1.14 Undo/Redo	This can be used to **Undo** or **Redo** a previous step.
	Undo Command - Previous step only. Ctrl Z or *Edit Menu→Undo.*
	   Mac CS6: Use the command Z *for Undo.*
	   Redo Command - If you do too many **Undos**, **Redo** them by pressing Ctrl Y
	   or *Edit Menu→Redo. Mac CS6: Use the* command Y *for undo.*

1.15 History	The **History Panel** is used to review the entire history of an opened session and will allow multiple **Undos**. **History Panel**: *Window Menu→History.*
Practice Exercise 6 *Undo, Redo, History*	1. *File Menu→Open→C:\Data\IllustratorCC-1\My Advertisment1.ai→* Open . 2. *Delete several items.* 3. *Now use the History, Undo, and Redo commands to change the image back to the original.*

1.16 Zooming	The following are several techniques used to zoom in and out:
	Zoom in: *Ctrl +* (**Mac CS6**: Use the **command +**).
	Zoom out: *Ctrl -* (**Mac CS6**: Use the **command -**).
	Full screen: *Ctrl 0* (**Mac CS6**: Use the **command 0**).
	Zoom out: *Hold Ctrl-Space Bar→With Left Mouse Click, Click, Click.*
	   (**Mac CS6**: Use the **command space bar**).
	Zoom in: *Hold: Ctrl Alt-Space Bar→With Left Mouse: Click, Click, Click.*
	   (**Mac CS6**: Use the **options command space bar**).

1.17 Zoom Tool	This will increase or decrease the **View Magnification** in the **Illustration Window**. Draw a box around the area to magnify. **Tip:** Use the *Alt Key* to Zoom out. (**Mac CS6:** Use the **option** key instead of the **Alt** key).
1.18 Navigator Panel	This will zoom in to view the entire area: *Window Menu →Navigator.* Navigator Zoom Area
Practice Exercise 7 Navigator	1. *File Menu →Open →File name: My Advertisement2.ai →Open.* 2. *Window Menu →Navigator.* 3. *Zoom in, Move the red box, and Zoom out.*
1.19 Properties Panel	This will allow you to change the characteristics of any object. *Window Menu →Properties →Select any object →Review the properties of the object.*
1.20 Control Panel	The **Control Panel** is located on the top of the interface. When you select a **Tool** the **Control Panel** options are available. *Window Menu →Control.*
1.21 Smart Guides	This displays green **Guidelines** automatically as you move 2 or more objects. Add a rectangle: *Rectangle Tool →Draw rectangle →Rectangle Tool →Draw the second rectangle and watch for the green Smart Guides.*
1.22 Rulers	**Rulers** are used to measure distances. Pull the guides out of the **Ruler** by dragging and placing them within the document. *View Menu →Rulers →Show/Hide Rulers.*
1.23 Guides	Hide or show **Guides** on the screen: *View Menu →Guides →Show.* To add **Guides**, drag the **Ruler Vertically** or **Horizontally** to the document. To move a **Guide** use the selection tool and move the **Guide** with the mouse. **Tip:** In order to move the **Guide** you must unlock it: *View Menu →Guides →Unlock.* Remove Guides: *View Menu →Guides →Clear Guides.*

Student Project A Artboard Tests	1. **Create an 8-1/2 x 11 Artboard:** *File Menu →New.*
	2. **Draw an Artboard:** *Artboard Tool.*
	3. **Delete and Artboard:** *Artboard Panel.*
	4. **Open-File:** *LogosFish and Wildlife.jpg.*
	5. **Zoom:** *Ctrl +, -, 0.*
	6. **Move Artboard:** *Hand Tool.*
	7. **Move one Artboard:** *Artboard Tool.*
	8. **Test the Navigator Panel:** *Window Menu →Navigator.*
	9. **Test the Smart Guides:** *Place Image.*
	    LogosFish and Wildlife2.
	    LogosFish and Wildlife3.
	   Tip: When opening, select both images using the *Ctrl or Shift Keys.*
	10. **Rulers:** *Turn on the Ruler.*
	11. **Guide:** *Add Guide to Artboard.*

1.24 Color Panel	*Window Menu→Color.* See the color picker below: **Tip: To expand the Color Panel**: *Click the menu icon→Show Options*
1.25 Color Picker	The **Color Picker** is located at the bottom of the **Tools Panel** (left side of the interface) and is used to define **Foreground** and **Border** colors. The **Foreground** color (color on top) is the default color used for tools such as **Paint Bucket** or **Paint Brush Tools**. The following will describe some of the icons located in the **Color Picker**: **Default Border and Foreground Colors** - By clicking on this button, the **Foreground** color will be set to black and the **Border** color will turn white. **Switch Foreground and Border Color** - When this button is pressed, the **Foreground** and **Border** color is **Switched** in order to draw with the default color. **Foreground and Border Color** - The box on top contains the **Foreground** color and is also the default color used by the system. The box under the **Foreground Border** color is available if you use the **Switch** button. **Foreground Color Picker** - This will open the **Foreground Color Picker** dialog box that defines the color. **In order to choose a different color:** *Double click on the Foreground box in the Color Picker (located at the bottom of the Tools Panel).* **Choose Color** - Grab this icon and move it around to choose a different color. **Web Safe Colors** Only Web Colors - Checking this will display only colors that are within the **Web Browsers** color range. This is referred to as the safe color range. **Choose Different Color Spectrums** - Move these controls to change the color spectrums.

New Color - The top portion is the **New Color** defined by moving the ◎ or ◁▷ icon.

Original Color current - The bottom portion is the color prior to using this tool.

Web Safe Warning - This symbol tells you the color chosen is *not* safe to use on a **Web Page.** If you use a color that is **Not Web Safe**, the final color may change or shift to a more standard supported color.

Out Of Gamut for Printing Warning ⚠ - This symbol tells you the color chosen is *not* safe to use for **Printed Material** and does not mix well with other standard ink colors. Therefore, if you use an **Out Of Gamut** color, the final color may change or shift to a more standard supported color.

Add To Swatches Add to Swatches - This will add the chosen **New Color** to the **Swatches Panel** for easy access and permanent storage. *Window Menu →Swatches.*

HSB Color Code H: 123 ° S: 91 % B: 89 % - This stands for **Hue**, **Saturation**, and **Brightness** and is a color model used to define specific colors in a spectrum.

RGB Color Code R: 20 G: 226 B: 30 - This stand for **Red**, **Green,** and **Blue.** It is a color definition system that ranges from 0 (low intensity) to 255 (high intensity) that defines specific colors. For example, if you enter R=255, G=0, and B=255 it will give you a true purple. However, if you reduce the intensity of Red to R=150, G=0, and B=255 you will get a blueish-purple color. See the practice exercise below to test this out.

Hexadecimal # 14e21e - This is a color definition based on a 16-bit numbering system and is used most often in web development. The 16-bit numbering system counts from "0 to f" (0,1,2,3,4,5,6,7,8,9,a,b,c,d,e,f). The **ff** represents high-intensity **Red**, **00** represents no **Green** added, and **99** represents lower-intensity **Blue.** The mixtures of these colors make up other colors. For example, **#ff0000** = pure red, **#0000ff** = pure blue, and **#ff00ff** = purple or a mixture of red and blue. **Tip:** In HTML web page code, **Hexadecimal** colors can be defined in the form of **<body bgcolor=#ff0099>**.

CMYK Color Code C: 68 % M: 0 % Y: 100 % K: 0 % - This stand for **Cyan**, **Magenta**, **Yellow,** and **Black.** It is used to define a specific color in a spectrum by mixing colors to define the desired color.

Practice Exercise 8 RGB	1. *Double-click on the Color Picker located at the bottom of the Tools Panel.* 2. *Create a purple color by entering the values in the RGB boxes below:* R: 255 R: 150 R: 255 G: 0 G: 0 G: 0 B: 255 B: 255 B: 150

Practice Exercise 9 Hexadecimal	1. ***Double-click on the Color Picker*** located at the bottom of the Tools **Panel.** 2. **Create a turquoise color by mixing green and blue:** *Example: #00ffff.* **To lighten the intensity of blue:** *Try: #00ff99.* 3. **Test It:** *Try a few of the colors below or make up your color:*

Color Name	Code	Color Name	Code	Color Name	Code
AliceBlue	#eff7ff	Gray52	#7a7777	MistyRose	#fde1dd
AntiqueWhite	#f9e8d2	Gray53	#7c7979	MistyRose2	#ead0cc

Practice Exercise 10 Web Safe Out Of Gamut	1. ***Double-click on the Color Picker*** located at the bottom of the Tools **Panel.** 2. ***Choose a different color by moving the choose color*** or spectrum **icon.** 3. ***Watch for the*** Not Web Safe or Out of Gamut warning icon. 4. ***When the icon appears, click on it to convert the color to a safe color.***

Section 2 - Optional Topics

1.26 Arrange	In order to **Arrange** two documents side by side, use the **Arrange** options. Also, you can make the document float by grabbing the document tab and dragging it to the middle of the screen. ***Open 2 documents →Window Menu →Arrange →Tile.*** **Tip**: In order to **Arrange** the documents to the tabs on the top, choose: **Consolidate All Windows.**
Practice Exercise 11 *Arrange*	Open two files and **Arrange** the files side-by-side: ***File Menu →Open →C:\Data\IllustratorCC-1\My Advertisement1.ai→*** `Open` . ***File Menu →Open →C:\Data\IllustratorCC-1\My Advertisement2.ai→*** `Open` . ***Window Menu →Arrange → Tile.*** ***Window Menu →Arrange → Consolidate All Windows.***
1.27 Workspace	The system will remember the layout of menus and panels using this feature. Some of the commonly used layouts are: **Workspace** Essentials (Default), and Essentials Classic. ***Switch Workspace (Located in the upper right corner of the interface)***
Practice Exercise 12 *Workspace*	1. ***Change the Workspace to Essentials Classic and back to Essentials: Switch Workspace →Essentials Classic.*** ***Switch Workspace →Essentials.*** 2. **New Workspace** - This creates a new custom **Workspace**. ***Switch Workspace →New Workspace →Name.*** 3. **Reset the Active Workspace to its default settings:** ***Window Menu →Workspace →Reset*** `Reset Essentials` . 4. **Delete Workspace -** ***Window Menu→ Workspace→Delete Workspace→*** ***(Delete your new workspace).***

1.28 Preferences	These are computer settings that change the behavior of a program.
	Preferences are located in: ***Edit Menu →Preferences.***
	    Mac: Illustrator Menu →Preferences.
	Some common Preferences include:
	1. **Display Start Screen:** ***Edit Menu →Preferences →General →***
	☑ Show The Home Screen When No Documents Are Open
	2. **Change the color of an entire interface:** ***Edit Menu →Preferences →User Interface →Brightness:*** **Lighter/Darker workspace.**
	
	    CS6 User Interface:
	3. **To adjust performance settings:** ***Edit Menu →Preferences →Performance.***
	4. **Change the default units of a system:** ***Edit Menu →Preferences →Units.***
	5. **Display Ruler:** ***Edit Menu →Preferences →General →*** ☑ Show/Hide Rulers

1.29 Keyboard Options	**Keyboard** combinations can be displayed or defined for **Tools** or **Menu Commands.** *Edit→Keyboard Shortcuts →(Choose a command).*
Practice Exercise 13 Keyboard Tools	View the **Tools** shortcuts: ***Edit Menu →*** ***Keyboard Shortcuts →*** ***Paintbrush.*** Notice there is no **Keyboard** command defined for **Paintbrush.** 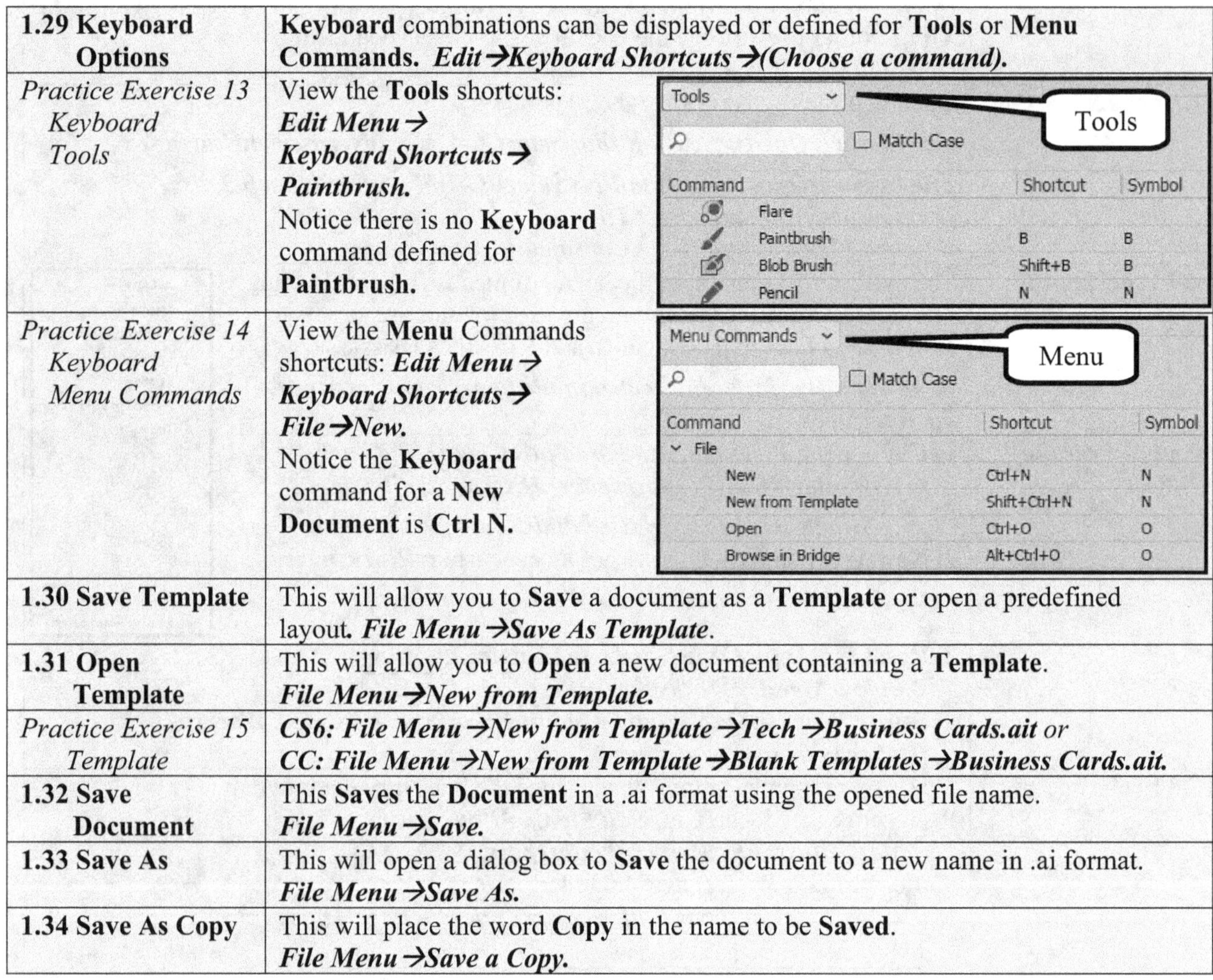
Practice Exercise 14 Keyboard Menu Commands	View the **Menu** Commands shortcuts: ***Edit Menu →*** ***Keyboard Shortcuts →*** ***File →New.*** Notice the **Keyboard** command for a **New Document** is **Ctrl N.**
1.30 Save Template	This will allow you to **Save** a document as a **Template** or open a predefined layout. *File Menu →Save As Template.*
1.31 Open Template	This will allow you to **Open** a new document containing a **Template**. *File Menu →New from Template.*
Practice Exercise 15 Template	***CS6: File Menu →New from Template →Tech →Business Cards.ait*** *or* ***CC: File Menu →New from Template →Blank Templates →Business Cards.ait.***
1.32 Save Document	This **Saves** the **Document** in a .ai format using the opened file name. *File Menu →Save.*
1.33 Save As	This will open a dialog box to **Save** the document to a new name in .ai format. *File Menu →Save As.*
1.34 Save As Copy	This will place the word **Copy** in the name to be **Saved.** *File Menu →Save a Copy.*

1.35 Browse In Bridge	The product **Bridge** is an **Adobe** program used to display graphic images in an easy-to-navigate interface. You can open a picture in **Illustrator** by double-clicking on a picture. To start **Bridge,** go to *File Menu→Browse in Bridge* or start the application from the **Windows** start button. There are many features available, but a few important ones are: 1. **Keywords** - *Right-click on an image→Info→Add Keywords*. 2. **Keyword Check Box** - After a keyword is added to the **Keyword Info Panel**, the checkbox is located in the **Keyword** or the **Filter Panel**. 3. **Search** - To **Search** the keyword, type the word in the search box located in the upper right corner. 4. **Thumbnail Size** - This is located on the bottom of the screen and is used to size the thumbnails. 5. **Preview Panel** - If the images are displaying a small thumbnail, the **Preview Panel** can be used to display it larger.
Practice Exercise 16 Adobe Bridge	The **Bridge** product is a very powerful technique used to view unopened files. You can assign attributes to files for searching and finding images. *File Menu →Browse in Bridge →Find Folder: IllustratorCC-1 →* *Open File: C:\Data\IllustratorCC-1\Rock Climb.ai* *by double-clicking on the file.*
1.36 Status Bar	**Zoom** - This feature is located in the lower left corner. **Artboard Page Number** - This lists each **Artboard** by number. **Active Tool** - This displays the active tool you are using.

Chapter 2 - Basic Shapes and Selection

These are the initial skills needed to add basic shapes to developing artwork. This includes selection tools, and drawing objects such as rectangles, arcs, and oval shapes, and is also the fundamental building block of the program.

Section 1 - Core Topics

Concept	Explanation / *Command String in italic*
2.1 Selection Tool	This will **Select** objects: ***When you select an object use the Shift Key to force the object to be proportional.*** Previous version icon:
2.2 Direct Selection Tool	This will select and move anchor points and corners within objects. It doesn't work with graphic images: Previous version icon **Tip**: You may need to click on a corner twice to move the endpoint.
Practice Exercise 17 *Rectangle*	**Draw a rectangle→ Add an anchor point → Select the Direct Selection Tool→ Click the anchor point and move the anchor point.**
2.3 Line Segment Tool	This draws straight **Line Segments**. **Shift Key** - This will draw the **Line** at 45-degree angles. **Alt Key** - This will draw the **Line** from the center out.
Practice Exercise 18 *Line Segment Tool*	***Hold the Shift Key to draw at 45 degrees. Hold Alt** (Mac CS6: Use the option Key) **to define the start point as the center point. Hold the Spacebar to move the line prior to releasing the left mouse.***
2.4 Arc Tool	This draws individual concave or convex curve segments. **To display the Arc Tool: *Choose the … Ellipse menu on the bottom of the Tools or Window Menu→ Workspace→ Essentials Classic.***
Practice Exercise 19 *Arc Tool*	***Hold the Shift Key (Mac: Use Option Key) to draw at 45 degrees. Hold Spacebar to move the line prior to releasing the left mouse.***
2.5 Rectangle Tool	This draws **Squares** and **Rectangles**. **Shift Key** - This will draw a perfect square. **Alt Key** - This will draw from the center out.
Practice Exercise 20 *Rectangle Tool*	***Hold the Alt Key** (Mac CS6: Use the option Key) **to draw centered. Hold the Shift Key to draw a proportional or a perfect square. Hold the Spacebar to move the rectangle prior to releasing the left mouse.***
2.6 Rounded Rectangle Tool	This draws **Squares** and **Rectangles** with rounded corners. **Shift Key** - This will draw a perfect square. **Alt Key** - This will draw from the center out. **Tip**: Use the **Rectangle Tool** and pull the inside handles to round the corners.

Practice Exercise 21 *Rounded* *Rectangle Tool*	***Hold the Alt Key** (Mac CS6: Use the option Key) **to draw centered. Hold the Shift Key to draw a proportional or perfect square. Hold the Spacebar to move the rectangle prior to releasing the left mouse.***
2.7 Ellipse Tool	This draws circles and ovals. **Shift Key** - This will draw a perfect circle. **Alt Key** - This will draw from the center out.
Practice Exercise 22 *Ellipse Tool*	***Hold the Alt Key** (Mac CS6: Use the option Key) **to draw centered. Hold the Shift Key to draw a proportional or perfect circle. Hold the Spacebar to move the ellipse prior to releasing the left mouse.***
2.8 Polygon Tool	This draws regular, multisided shapes. **Shift Key** - This will draw a perfect **Polygon**. **Alt Key** - This will draw from the center out.
Practice Exercise 23 *Polygon Tool*	***Hold the Alt Key** (Mac CS6: Use the option Key) **to draw with tighter edges. Hold the Shift Key to draw a proportional or a perfect polygon. Hold the Spacebar to move the polygon prior to releasing the left mouse.***
2.9 Star Tool	This draws **Stars**. **Shift Key** - This will draw a perfect **Star**. **Alt Key** - This will draw from the center out.
Practice Exercise 25 *Star Tool*	***Hold the Alt Key to draw centered. Hold the Shift Key to draw it perfectly straight. Hold the Spacebar to move the star prior to releasing the left mouse.***
2.10 Flare Tool	This creates **Lens-Flare** or **Solar-Flare** like effects. Previous version icon:
Practice Exercise 26 *Flare Tool*	***Draw two Flare objects to see how the second one interacts with the first one.***
2.11 Arrange	**Arranges** objects on top or under multiple shapes.
Practice Exercise 27 *Arrange*	1. ***Draw the following using the Drawing Tools.*** 2. ***Arrange the objects according to the drawing.*** 3. ***Object Menu →Arrange or Right-click →Arrange.***
2.12 Copy Image	Holding the **Alt** key down will **Copy** an **Image**.
Practice Exercise 28 *Copy*	***Select Object →Hold Alt Key →Drag n' Drop →Let go of the Alt Key.*** (Mac CS6: Use the option Key) **Tip**: Don't let go of the **Alt Key** before you let go of the **Mouse Button**.
2.13 Adjust **Proportional**	This will ensure the object will remain **Proportional**.
Practice Exercise 29 *Corner Handles*	***Select Object → Hold Shift Key→Drag corner handles.***
2.14 Shape **Adjustments**	This includes **Anchor Points, Paths Between Anchor Points, Center Points, End Points, and Rotational Handles**.
2.15 Grouping **Options**	This will group multiple objects. To move the **Grouped objects,** select any object in the **Group** and move it.

Practice Exercise 30 *Group*	Group the following objects together. Then, use **the Group Selection Tool** to move one of the objects. ***Select objects → Object Menu → Group.***
2.16 Transform Object	This will **Transform** an **Object**. You will be able to Move, Rotate, Reflect, Scale, or Shear an object.
Practice Exercise 31 *Transform*	Draw the following using the ***Shift*** and the ***Alt Keys*** to adjust the object. *(Mac CS6: Use the Command Key)* ***Window Menu → Transform*** *or* ***Object Menu → Transform.*** ***Or: Objects Menu → Transform.***
2.17 Reflect	This will reflect an image either vertically or horizontally.
Practice Exercise 32 *Reflect*	Reflect the grouped object using the Vertical reflection: ***Select object → Object Menu → Transform → Reflect.***
Student Project B *BBC Logo*	This will use the **Rectangle** and **Text Tool** to draw the **BBC** object: ***When drawing the rectangle, use the Shift Key to draw a perfect square and the Alt Key to make a copy of the squares.***
Student Project C *Target Logo*	This will use the **Ellipse Tool** and the **Arrange** feature to draw the object. ***Use the Shift Key along with the Arrow Keys to fine-tune the circle position.*** **Tip**: Use guides to measure distance and use the center ellipse feature (alt).
Student Project D *Domino's Pizza Logo*	This will use the **Rectangle Tool, Ellipse Tool, and Rotation Tool.** ***Use the Shift for a proportional layout, and Arrow Keys to fine-tune the position.***
Student Project E *Adidas Logo*	This will use the **Rectangle Tool, Text Tool, Rotation Tool, and Arrange Panel.** ***Use "Century Gothic" Font to match the style of the word "adidas."***
Student Project F *Star Logo*	This uses the **Rounded Rectangle Tool, Star Tool, and Direct Select Tool to change the shape of the star.** ***Grab the center anchor points of the star using the Direct Select Tool.*** **Tip:** Use the **Alt Key** to draw the star to get a perfect star shape.
Student Project G *CC Logo*	This uses the **Ellipse Tool**, shift to draw the circles proportional, and the **Rectangle Tool. Pobbible Solution:**
2.18 Magic Wand Tool	This will **Select** objects with similar attributes: **Tip:** Notice when you select one rectangle, both rectangles are selected. *Mac: Use Object Menu → Group.* Previous version icon:
Practice Exercise 33 *Magic Wand*	***Draw 2 rectangles → Magic Wand Tool → Select one rectangle → Use arrows to move images.***
2.19 Lasso Tool	This will draw points around an object to select it. Previous version icon:

2.20 Group Selection Tool	This will **Select** objects within groups. Previous version icon: First, Group 2 objects, choose the Group Selection Tool, then elect a single object in the group. *Mac:* ***Use Object Menu → Group***.	
Practice Exercise 34 *Group Rectangles*	1. ***Draw 2 rectangles using the Rectangle Tool.*** 2. ***Selection Tool → Shift-select multiple objects → Right-click → Group.*** 3. ***Use Group Selection Tool to select objects within a group.***	

Student Project H – Other Logos

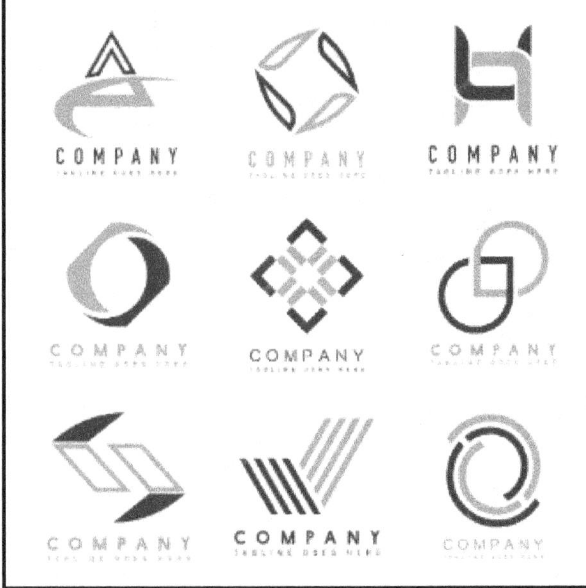

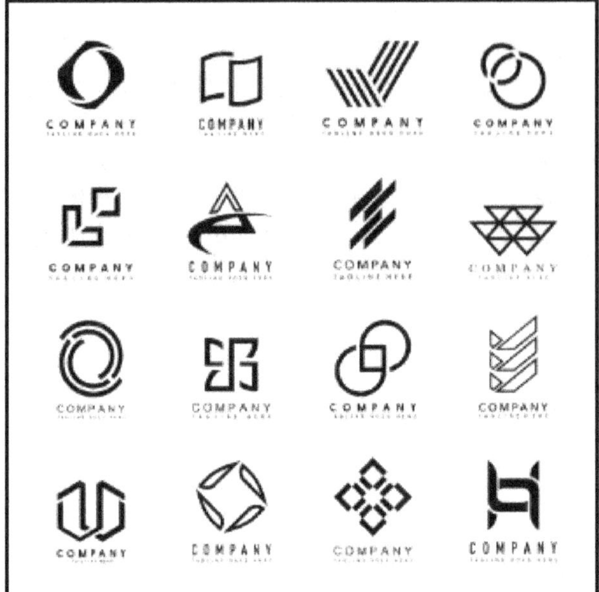

Section 2 - Optional Topics

2.21 Select Similar Objects	This option is located in the **Control Panel** is located on the top of the interface under the menus. **Tip**: To open the **Control Panel:** *Window Menu* → ✓ Control . Options available: All, Fill Color, Stoke color, Fill and Stroke color, Stroke Weight, Opacity, and Appearance. CS6: Icon:	✓ All Fill Color Stroke Color Fill & Stroke Color Stroke Weight Opacity Graphic Style Appearance Appearance Attribute Shape
Practice Exercise 35 Rectangle Tool	1. *Add two rectangles* → **Rectangle Tool.** 2. Change the Stroke (border-width): *Select Object* → *Window Menu* → *Stroke* → *Weight: 5 Pts* Weight: ⌄ 5 pt 3. *Selection Tool* → *Select one rectangle* → *Upper right corner on the bar* → *Select similar objects* → *Stroke Width.* **Tip: Illustrator CS6** does not have all options compared to **Illustrator CC.**	
2.22 Menu Selection	This will select objects that are similar. **CC Options** *Select Menu* → *Object.*	All on Same Layers Direction Handles Bristle Brush Strokes Brush Strokes Clipping Masks Stray Points All Text Objects Point Type Objects Area Type Objects
Practice Exercise 36 Text Tool	1. Create 2 Text Boxes: **T** *Text Tool* → *Draw Box* → *(Type some text in the Text Box).* **CS6 Options** 2a. CC: *Select Menu* → *Object* → *All Text Objects.* 2b. CS6: *Select Menu* → *Object* → *Text Objects.* **Tip:** CS6 has a different list of options. All on Same Layers / Direction Handles / Not Aligned to Pixel Grid / Bristle Brush Strokes / Brush Strokes / Clipping Masks / Stray Points / Text Objects	
2.23 Drawing Modes **CS6+**	This will **Draw Normal, Draw Behind** This will draw in front (Draw Normal). This will draw behind an object.	
Practice Exercise 37 Drawing Modes	This will use the **Paint Brush** or **Line Segment Tools.** *Draw a line* → *Draw Behind* → *Change Stroke color* → *Draw over the line segment.*	
2.24 Spiral Tool	This draws or spirals an image either clockwise or counterclockwise. Previous version icon:	
2.25 Rectangular Grid Tool	This draws **Rectangular grids**. Previous version icon:	

2.26 Polar Grid Tool	This draws **Circular Chart Grids**. Previous version icon:	
2.27 Live Corner Options	This activates the **Live Corners** feature and will allow you to adjust the square corners to rounded corners. Supported in **IllustratorCC+**. **Tip**: To view this feature: *View Menu → Show corner annotation.*	
Practice Exercise 38 Direct Select	***Draw Rectangle → Selection Tool → Select-Object → Choose Direct Select Tool and a small dot will appear near the corner → drag the dot to create a line corner.***	

Chapter 3 - Custom Paths

You will need to draw a **Custom Path** in order to provide the contour needed to shape your design. Drawing paths include **Pen Tools** and the **Pencil Tools**.

Concept	Explanation / *Command String in italic*
3.1 Pen Tool	This draws straight and curved lines: Use the **Alt Key** (**Mac CS6:** *Use the option Key*) to switch to the convert anchor point. ***Click point 1 → Click Point 2 → Don't let go of the mouse button → Hold the Alt Key and move the direction of the extended line → Click a point*** **Tip:** Use **Backspace Key** to **Undo.** Tip: The arc does not change direction. **Mac CS6:** Use the **option Key**. Previous version icon:
Practice Exercise 39 Pin Tool	This draws straight lines: ***Pen Tool → Click → Click → Click → Click.***
Practice Exercise 40 Fill	This will **Fill** the pen area: ***Select object →*** ***Make sure the fill box is on top. Double-click to change color.***
3.2 Add Anchor Point Tool	This adds **Anchor Points** to paths. Previous version icon:
Practice Exercise 41 Add Anchor Point	***Rectangle Tool → Draw a square → Add Anchor Point Tool → Add two anchor points to the edge → Pen Tool → Click on a corner.***
3.3 Delete Anchor Point	This **Deletes Anchor Points** on paths. Previous version icon:
3.4 Convert Anchor Point	This changes smooth points to corner points and vice versa. ***Hold the Shift Key to move it a specific distance. Double-click on the corner.***
Practice Exercise 42 Convert	1. ***Rectangle Tool → Draw a square.*** 2. ***Pen Tool → Click the corner.*** 3. ***Convert Anchor Point Tool → Round the corner.***

3.5 Creating Curves	This will create a **Curved** object:
Practice Exercise 43 Pin Tool	***Pen Tool→ Click 1 → Click 2 hold and drag down → Click 3 hold and drag up.***
3.6 Fill Pen Area	The fill color on top will color the crossover anchor points.
3.7 Unfill Pen Area	The stroke color on top will create a single path.
3.8 Bezier Curves	The curve was created with **Pen Tool**.
Student Project I Pen Tool	***Draw the smile, similar to the example, using the Pen Tool.***
Student Project J Pen Tool	***Draw the graph, similar to the example, using the Pen Tool.***
Student Project K Create Logo	***Use the Rectangle Tool, Ellipse Tool, and Pen Tools to create the Logo. See example:***
Student Project L Bezier Curves	***Draw several Bezier Curves and place text on the cup. The curve should follow the contour of the cup's rounded edge.***
Student Project M MNML Logo	***Use the Rectangle and Pen Tool to create the logo. Notice the "N" in white of the MNML.***
3.9 Path Formatting Tools	This will show some of the **Path Formatting Tools**.
Practice Exercise 44 Variable Width	**Brushes:** *Window Menu →Brush Definition* **Variable Width Profile:** *Options bar (Located on the top of the screen).* **Stroke Weight:** *Window Menu → Stroke.*
Practice Exercise 45 Clouds	***Create Clouds freehand using the Pencil Tool. Be sure to change the tool direction.***

3.10 Pen Tool With ALT	This will use the **Alt Key** (Mac CS6: Use the option Key) to change the direction of the path.
Practice Exercise 46 Cloud Segments	This creates clouds changing direction: 1. ***Draw the first segment*** 2. ***Use Alt Key (Mac CS6: Use the option Key) to change direction*** 3. ***Continue to draw segments.***
Practice Exercise 47 Pin Tool	***Create Clouds freehand using the Pencil Tool. Be sure to change the tool direction.***
3.11 Direct Select Tool	This is used to change the object by adding and moving the anchor points. You may need to click twice on the **Anchor** point to move the endpoint.
Practice Exercise 48 Anchor Point	This uses **Pen +** to add an anchor and the **ct Select** to move the anchor point. ***Rectangle Tool → Draw a rectangle → Add Anchor Point Tool → Add Anchor points → Direct Selection Tool → Move anchor points.***
Practice Exercise 49 Anchor Point	Change **Anchor Points** on a house: ***Draw the roof of a house or barn. Add an anchor point and stretch the anchor point using the Direct Selection Tool.***
Practice Exercise 50 Pin Tool	Draw the following shape using the **Pen Tool**.
Student Project N Sketch	1. ***File Tab → Open → Sketch.ai*** 2. ***Use the Pen Tool and draw anchor points on the Top, Bottom, Left and Right edges.*** 3. ***Set the transparency to 50% (Window Menu → Transparency).*** 4. ***Use the direct select Tool to adjust the anchor point by stretching the anchor point lines.***

Chapter 4 - Drawing Tools

Test out the most common **Drawing Tools**.

Concept	Explanation / *Command String in italic*
4.1 Shaper Tool	His allows you to draw freehand the result will turn into a perfect circle or square adjust existing shapes. **Tip**: This is a new tool and is supported in CC+
Practice Exercise 51 Shaper Tool CC+	Draw the following freehand shapes:
4.2 Pencil Tool	This draws a free-form line. Previous version icon: Keyboard Command: N
Practice Exercise 52 Pencil Tool	***Draw using the Pencil tool.***
4.3 Smoothing Tool	This draws **Smooth** corners on straight edges. Previous version icon:
Practice Exercise 53 Smooth Corners	***Draw rectangle → Smooth corners.***
4.4 Path Eraser Tool	This **Erases Paths** and **Anchor points** from the object. Previous version icon:
Practice Exercise 54 Path Eraser Tool	***Draw Pencil → Path Eraser Tool.***
4.5 Join Tool CC+	This joins 2 lines that are almost intersecting. **Tip**: This is a new tool and is supported in CC+.
Practice Exercise 55 Join	***Draw 2 lines with the ends close together →Join Tool → Draw near the intersection point → Release the mouse button.*** 1. Draw two lines 2. Draw using Join Tool 3. The Result
4.6 Two Modes to view the end result of the Pencil Tool.	The fill color on top will color the crossover anchor points. The stroke color on top will create a single path.

Practice Exercise 56 *Pencil Tool*	Use the **Pencil Tool** to draw the following: 1. ***Draw Ellipse.*** 2. ***Use the Pencil Tool to draw cloud edges.***
Practice Exercise 57 *Draw A Sun*	Draw a **Sun**: 1. ***Draw a yellow circle.*** 2. ***Use the Pencil Tool to draw the edges.***
4.7 Match Path Color	As you draw the path above a rectangle using the **Pen Tool**, it will expand and match the color.
Practice Exercise 58 *Match Path* *Color*	***Draw a green rectangle (closed Shape) →Select the object→Use the Pencil Tool and draw near the edge of the rectangle. It will take on the color of the rectangle.***
Student Project O *Draw House*	Draw the following using the **Tools** provided. ***Draw the sky and mountain first, then, draw the foreground objects.***
4.8 Paint Brush Tool	This draws freehand, calligraphic lines, as well as patterns and bristles brush strokes. ***Use the Brush definitions in the Brush Panel→ Choose variable width profiles in brush options.*** Previous version icon:
Practice Exercise 59 *Paint Brush*	This uses the **Paintbrush Tools** to draw the objects to the right. ***Open the Brushes Panel: Window Menu→ Brushes→ More→ Open Brush Library→ Artistic→ Artistic Paintbrush.***
Student Project P *Draw Logo*	***To draw this logo, use the Line Segment Tool and change the Variable Width Profile to:*** ***and the Stroke to: 25 pt. Use the Alt Key to make copies and the Rectangle Tool.***
4.9 Blob Brush Tool	This draws paths that automatically expand and merge calligraphic brush paths that share the same color and are adjacent in the stacking order. Previous version icon: The shift draws paths at 45 degrees. **Tip:** Use the **[ ] Key**s to increase and decrease the brush size.

Practice Exercise 60 *Blob Brush*	**Use the Blob Brush Tools to draw the following.** **Draw Blob Brush → Select-Object → Effects Menu → Stylize →** **Outer Glow.**	
4.10 Eraser **Tool**	This **Erases** object lines. Previous version icon:	
Practice Exercise 61 *Eraser Tool*	**Select an object and erase it.**	
4.11 Scissors Tool	This slices an object at the anchor points. Previous version icon:	
Practice Exercise 62 *Scissor Tool*	**Add a Star → Scissor Tool → Click on anchor points → Move** **apart.**	
4.12 Knife Tool	This cuts up an object. Previous version icon:	
Practice Exercise 63 *Knife Tool*	**The cut can be done anywhere on the object.**	
Practice Exercise 64 *Drawing Tools*	**Test out each Drawing Tool by selecting one and** **drawing it on an Artboard.**	
4.13 Path And Line **Formatting**	The following tools can be used with the format lines and paths: **Fill, Stroke, Variable With Profile, Styles.**	
Practice Exercise 65	**Formatting Tools -Test out the Formatting Tools.**	
Student Project Q *Initials*	*Write your initials using different artistic brushes.* Uniform Artistic_Ink *More Options →Open Brush* *Library →*	

Practice Exercise 66 – Draw Artistic Brush Strokes

Draw the following using a Paintbrush Tool and change the brushes to view the effect. Paintbrush Tool→Brush Definition drop-down→Brush Libraries Menu →Artistic.

Style Artistic Effects

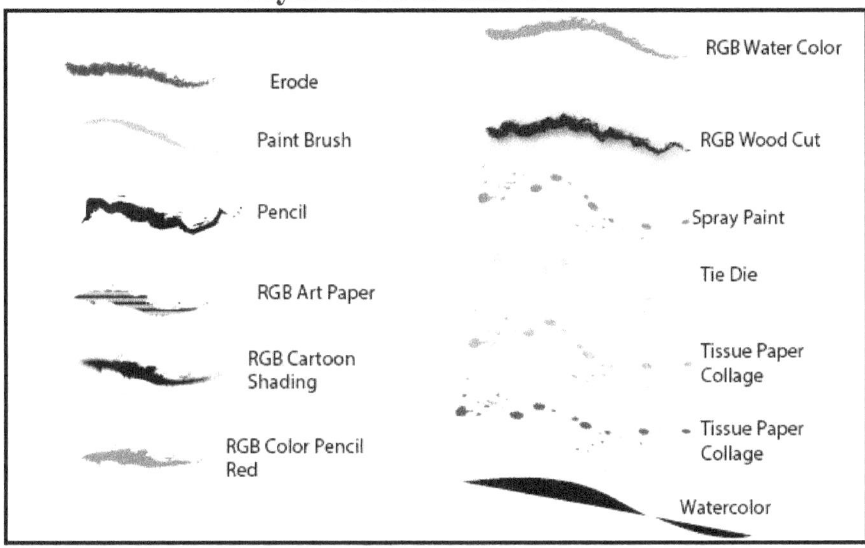

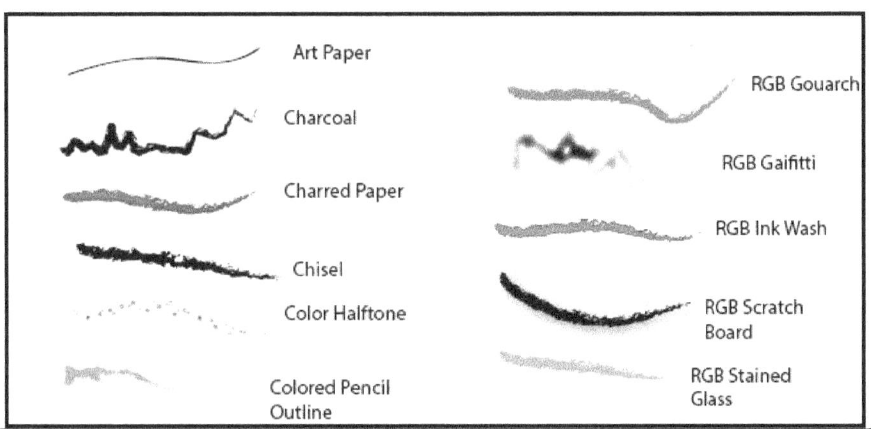

Chapter 5 - Text

We will use the **Text Tool** in a variety of ways including putting text in graphics objects.

Section 1 - Core Topics

Concept	Explanation / *Command String in italic*
5.1 Change Case	*Type Menu* → *Change Case.*
5.2 Text Background Box	Normally when you select a **Text Box** and choose **Fill** or **Stroke**, it will modify the actual text, not the **Text Box**. In order to change the background color behind the text, you need to use the ▷ **Direct Select Tool.** Be sure to select the corner edge so you can format it as desired (see below).
Practice Exercise 67 Fill	To fill the background of the text box: ***Make sure nothing is selected*** → ▷ ***Direct Select Tool*** → ***Select the corner of the Text Box*** → ***Fill: (Change the color).*** This is text in a text box — Select the corner of This is text in a text box — Incorrect selection.
5.3 Type Tool	T This creates individual **Type** containers to enter text. Previous version icon: T
Practice Exercise 68 Type Tool	***Select the Type Tool*** → ***Draw a box on the Artboard*** → ***Type text.***
5.4 Area Type Tool	This allows one to type text in a contained object**.** Click on the inside edge of the object, not the middle. Previous version icon:
Practice Exercise 69 Area Type Tool	***Draw an enclosed area with Pencil Tool*** → ***Select the Area Type Tool*** → ***Type Text.***
5.5 Type On A Path Tool	Text can be typed on a curved path by using a pen, pencil, or surface on an object. Previous version icon:
Practice Exercise 70 Type On A Path	***Draw a Spiral using the Spiral Tool*** → ***Select the Type on a Path Tool*** → ***Click on the path*** → ***Type the text.***
5.6 Vertical Type Tool	↓T This is similar to the **Type Tool**, but the text is entered vertically. Previous version icon: ↓T
Practice Exercise 71 Vertical Type	***Select the Vertical Type Tool*** → ***Draw a box on the Artboard*** → ***Type text.***
5.7 Vertical Area Type Tool	↓T This is similar to the **Area Type Tool**, but the text is entered vertically. Previous version icon:
Practice Exercise 72 Vertical Area	***Select the Vertical Area Type Tool*** → ***Draw a box on the Artboard*** → ***Type text.***

5.8 Vertical Type On A Path Tool	This is similar to the **"Type On a Path" Tool**, but the text is entered vertically. Previous version icon:	
Practice Exercise 73 Vertical Type On A Path Tool	***Draw an object on the Artboard→ Select the Vertical Type On A Path Tool→ Type text.***	
Practice Exercise 74 Symbols Library	This draws a curved text box over an object. ***Sunflower: Window Menu→ Symbols→More Options*** ≡ **→ *Open Symbol Library→ Flowers.***	
5.9 Text Path Formatting Effects	This draws a **Rainbow, Skew, Stair Step, 3D Ribbon and, Gravity.** *Type Menu→Type on a Path→Skew.* **Tip**: Use **Type On A Path.** **Tip:** You can't use a regular **Type Tool**, only use **Type on a Path Tool.**	
5.10 3d Ribbon	This draws 3D objects.	
Practice Exercise 75 Type On A Path	***Draw an ellipse→ Type on a Path Tool→ Type text on the curve→ Select text→ Type Menu→ Type on a Path→ 3D Ribbon.***	
Practice Exercise 76 Type On A Path	This uses the **Type On A Path Tool.** 1. ***Draw a path using the Pen Tool***s. 2. ***Use the Type on a Path Tool.***	
5.11 Type on a Path Alignments Options	This uses **Baseline, Ascender, Descender, Center, and Flip**: *Type Menu→Type on a Path→ Type on a Path Options*.	
Practice Exercise 77 Alignment Baseline Tool	Use the **Alignment Baseline Tool** to adjust the **Alignment.**	
5.12 Character Panel	This uses the **Font Family, Font Style, Font Size, Leading, Kerning, and Tracking for Selected Characters.**	
5.13 Text Formatting	This uses the **Font Family, Font Style, Font Size, Leading, Kerning, Tracking for Selected Characters, Vertical Scale, Horizontal Scale, Baseline Shift, Rotation, All Caps, Small Caps, Supper-Scripts, Sub-Scripts, Underline, and Strike-Through.**	
5.14 Character Formatting	*Type Tool→Options Menu →Character: option* The following options are available: **Vertical Scale, Horizontal Scale, Baseline Shift, Rotation, All Caps, Small Caps, Super-Scripts, Sub-Scripts, Underline, and Strike-Through.**	

5.15 Import Text	This will **Place** or **Import** text into **Illustrator**.
Practice Exercise 78 Import	This **Imports** text by placing text: *File Menu →Place → Give My Regards to Broadway.txt.*
5.16 Text Styles	These are the **Paragraph** and **Character Styles**. **Tip**: To change the default font type, change the font type in the **Character Styles** panel. *Window Menu →Type →Character Styles →Normal Character Style →Basic Character Formats →Font Family.*
5.17 Typographic Characters	*These are Special Characters.* 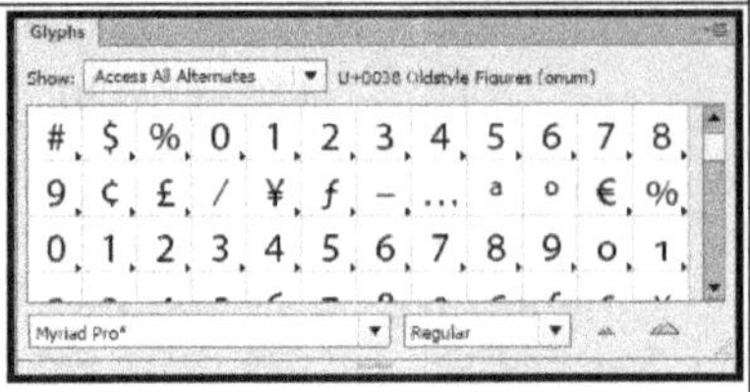
Practice Exercise 79 Typographic Characters	*Type Menu →Glyphs, Glyphs Panel.*
Student Project R 3D Effects	Project: *Create the following:*  1. *Ellipse tool →Draw a circle.* 2. *Type on a Path tool →Type the word "You" multiple times.* 3. *Type Menu →Type on a Path →3D Ribbon.* 4. *Make a copy of the ellipse →Resize ellipse → Type the text "are."* 5. *Make a copy of the ellipse →Resize ellipse → Type the text "my."* 6. *Insert the image: File Menu →Place → C:\Data\IllustratorCC-1\Heart1.jpg* *Test It: Test some of the other effects in the Type Menu →Text on a Path →(choose option).*
Student Project S Logo	*Test out the Character Formatting Tools. Click the* Character: *in the type toolbar. Use Bell MT* 
Student Project T Optional	*Create one graphic using the Pen Tool. Then, use the Alt to copy the image and the Transform Tool to reflect the image.* **Tip:** *Zoom into the image and trace the black graphic image.* 

Section 2 - Optional Topics

5.18 Threaded Text	This will tie or hook together 2 or more **TextBoxes**. Red (lower right corner) to thread. Single-click on the red box to unthread.
Practice Exercise 80 *Threads*	***Thread Text:*** ***File Menu→Place→*** ***Balanced Diet.docx→*** ☑ ***Remove Text*** ***Formatting.***
5.19 Touch Type Tool **CC+**	This is an intuitive way to adjust the scaling, position, and rotation of individual characters in the text. It can be used to create **Drop Caps** for paragraphs. **Tip**: This is a new tool and is supported in CC.
Practice Exercise 81 *Touch Type Tool*	*Use the Type Tool and enter some text→ Touch Type Tool→ Click on a letter and expand the letter using the double arrows.*
Practice Exercise 82 *Type Tools*	**Use the Object Tools to draw the following and type some text in each object.** 1. *Star Tool→Draw a Star object.* 2. *Format the star by removing the background.* 3. *Type Tool→Select object →(Type the desired text).* ***Test It: Try out some of the other objects.***
5.20 Distort Text w / Envelopes	This uses **Envelopes** to produce striking advertisements with warped text.
Practice Exercise 83 *Warp Text*	Envelope Options Make with Warp. ***Object Menu→ Envelope Distort→ Make with Warp.***
5.21 Object Rasterize	This will convert the text into a graphic image. *Select Text→Object Menu→Rasterize*

Section 3 – Character and Paragraph Formatting

This section covers all character formatting options.

5.22 Type Options Panel

When you select the [T Type Tool] **Type Tool**, the following Options panel will appear on top of the interface under the menu dropdown.

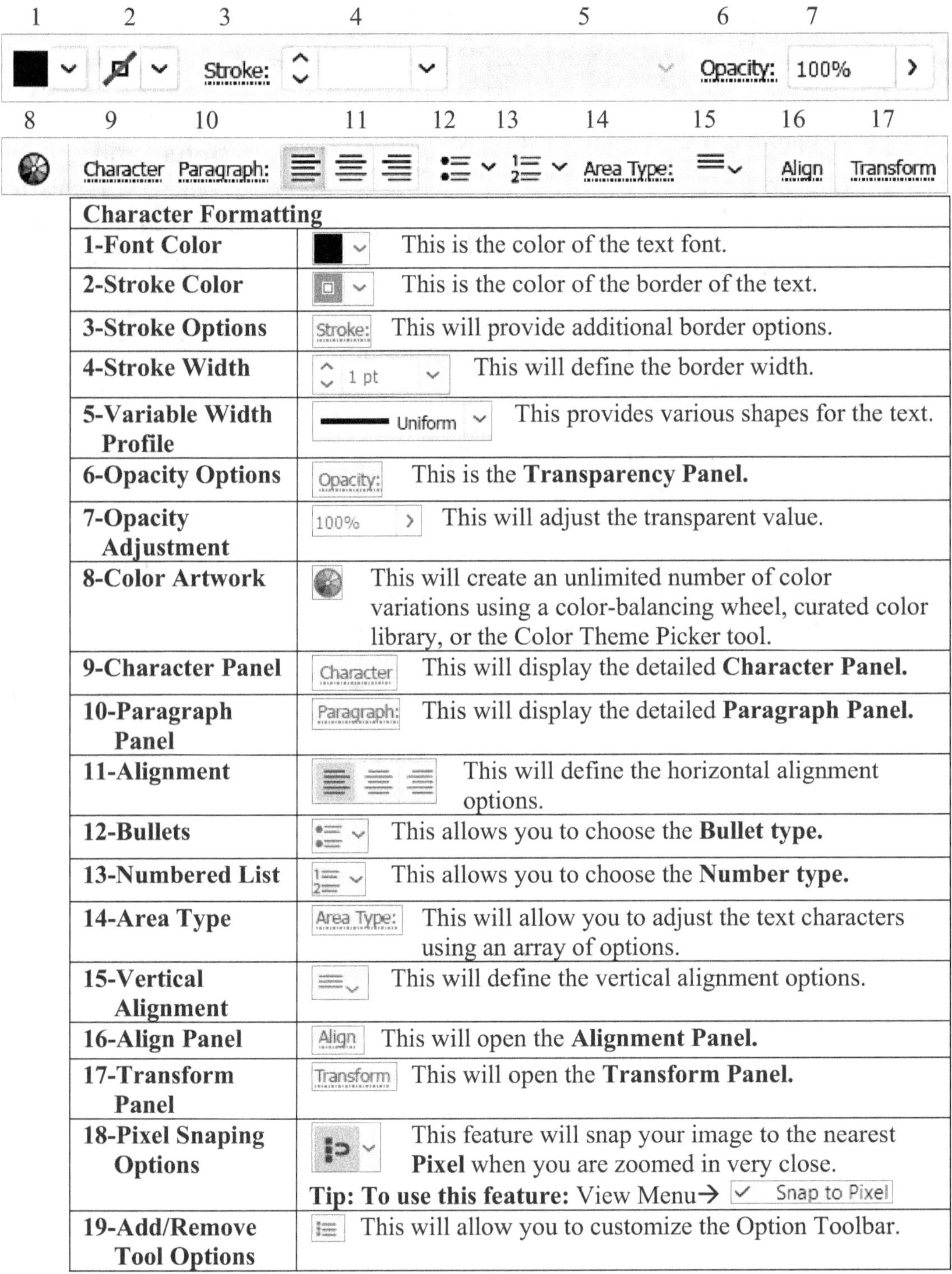

Character Formatting		
1-Font Color		This is the color of the text font.
2-Stroke Color		This is the color of the border of the text.
3-Stroke Options	Stroke:	This will provide additional border options.
4-Stroke Width	1 pt	This will define the border width.
5-Variable Width Profile	Uniform	This provides various shapes for the text.
6-Opacity Options	Opacity:	This is the **Transparency Panel.**
7-Opacity Adjustment	100%	This will adjust the transparent value.
8-Color Artwork		This will create an unlimited number of color variations using a color-balancing wheel, curated color library, or the Color Theme Picker tool.
9-Character Panel	Character	This will display the detailed **Character Panel.**
10-Paragraph Panel	Paragraph:	This will display the detailed **Paragraph Panel.**
11-Alignment		This will define the horizontal alignment options.
12-Bullets		This allows you to choose the **Bullet type.**
13-Numbered List		This allows you to choose the **Number type.**
14-Area Type	Area Type:	This will allow you to adjust the text characters using an array of options.
15-Vertical Alignment		This will define the vertical alignment options.
16-Align Panel	Align	This will open the **Alignment Panel.**
17-Transform Panel	Transform	This will open the **Transform Panel.**
18-Pixel Snaping Options		This feature will snap your image to the nearest **Pixel** when you are zoomed in very close. **Tip: To use this feature:** View Menu→ ✓ Snap to Pixel
19-Add/Remove Tool Options		This will allow you to customize the Option Toolbar.

5.23 Character Panel

When you choose the **Type Tool**, the top changes to the **Character Format Controls**. Click on this

Character button to switch to the **Character Panel**.

Open Illustrator and create a text box: *Type tool→draw the text box in Illustrator →*

Click Character *(located in the options toolbar on the top under the menu system.*

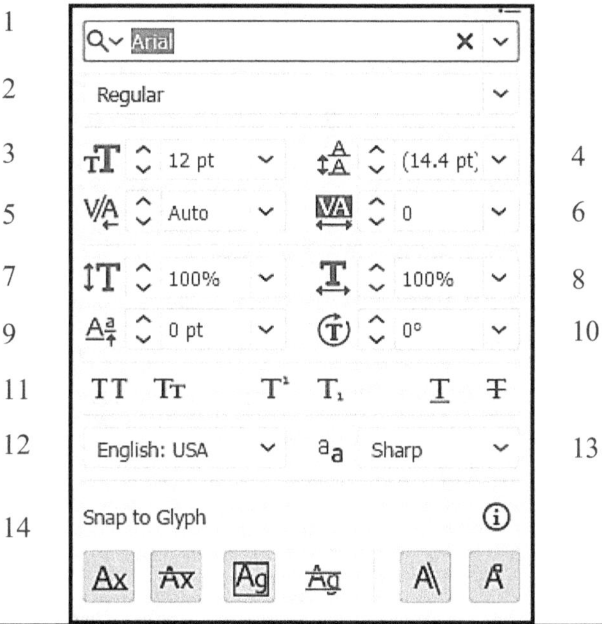

1- Font Family	These are **Fonts** such as **Arial, Times New Roman**, etc.
2-Character Type	This displays the **Character type** such as **Regular, Italic, Bold, and Bold Italic.**
3-Font Size	This allows you to change the **Font Size**. **Tip:** The value can be typed in, or choose from the pull-down menu.
4-Leading	This adjusts the spacing between words on two rows. *W1 →Enter Key →W2 →Select both →Change the Leading value*.
5-Kerning	This will adjust a specified **distance between characters** that overlap. For example, WA can be kerned so the W and A fit closer together. This is used to better fit a title on a line by bringing all characters closer together. To turn it off: choose 0. Some common kerning examples are: **LA, P., To, Tr, Ta, Tu, Te, Ty, Wa, WA, We, Wo, Ya, and Yo.**
Practice Exercise 84 Kerning	*Type WA →Change font size to 72 pts →Place the cursor between the text W|A →Change kerning to -50.*

5a. **Kerning Metrics**	This depends on **Kern pairs AP, AF, AT, FA, LV, and LW**. **Metric Kerning** is included in most fonts.
5b. **Kerning Optical**	This is useful for characters with different font types. When using different types of faces or sizes, **Optical Kerning** is best.
6-Tracking	This loosens or tightens a block of text, but will not affect the **Kerning**.
Practice Exercise 85 Tracking	*Type: WA →Change font size to 72 pts →Select both letters WA →Change Tracking to -50.*
7-Vertical Scale	This will scale the text larger or smaller in a **vertical** direction.
Practice Exercise 86 Vertical Scale	*Type the word: TEST →Select the text →Change the vertical scale value.*
8-Horizontal Scale	This will scale the text larger or smaller in a **horizontal** direction.
Practice Exercise 87 Horizontal Scale	*Type the word: TEST →Select the text →Change the horizontal scale value.*
9-Baseline Shift	This will move a selected character up or down a specific distance from the **Baseline**. (**2**nd shifts upward and **Log$_{23}$** shifts downward).
Practice Exercise 88 Baseline Shift	*Type the word: Log23 →Select 23 →change the baseline shift value.*
10-Character Rotation	This will **Rotate** the characters.
11-Character Adjustment	This will include **All Caps, Small Caps, Supper-Scripts, Sub-Scripts, Underlines, and Strike-Through.**
12-Language	This will change to a different **Language**.
13-Set the Anti-Aliasing Method	This will define the **Anti-Aliasing** method to the following: None, Sharp, Crisp, or Strong.
14-Snap To Glyth	This will snap to Glyth characters in different ways.

5.24 Paragraph Panel

When you choose the **Type Tool**, the top changes to the **Character Format Controls**. Click on this

Paragraph: button to switch to the **Paragraph Panel**.

Open Illustrator and create a text box: *Type tool→draw the text box in Illustrator →*

Click Paragraph: *(located in the options toolbar on the top under the menu system.*

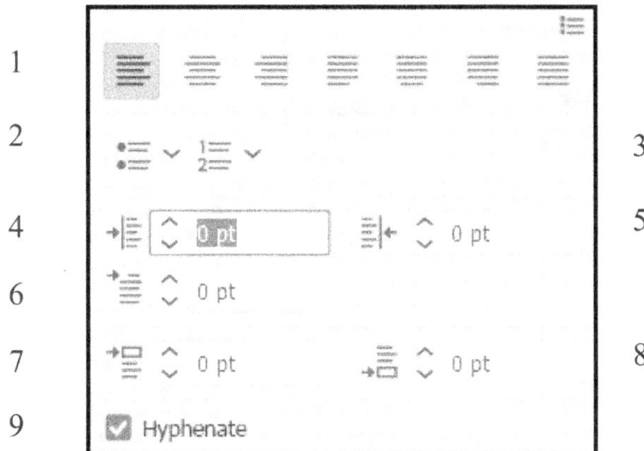

1-Alignment Options	This will **Align** your text.	
2-Bulleted List	This puts a **Bulleted List** in front of the selected text.	
3-Numbered List	This puts a **Numbered List** in front of the selected text.	
4-Left Indent	This **Indents** a paragraph by a specific amount on the **Left** which affects the entire paragraph.	
5-Right Indent	This **Indents** a paragraph by a specific amount on the **Right** which affects the entire paragraph.	
6-First line left indent	This will affect only the **First Line**.	
7-Space Before Paragraph	These are **Spaces** placed **Before Paragraphs** by a certain specified amount.	
8-Space After Paragraph	These are **Spaces** placed **After** a **Paragraph** by a specified amount.	
9-Hyphenate	This turns on the ability to continue a word on the next line. Example: think-ing.	

Chapter 6 - Customized Objects

In this chapter, you will use tools to adjust graphics pictures, objects, and manipulate the images.

Section 1 - Core Topics

Concept	Explanation / *Command String in italic*
6.1 Measure Tool	This **Measures** the distance between two points. Previous version icon:
Practice Exercise 89 *Measure Tool*	This will align anchor points or objects. ***Draw two objects →Select the Measure Tool →click on the first image and then click on the second image.***
6.2 Align Panel	***Window Menu → Align Panel*** Align → ***Align*** ***Anchor Points.***
Student Project U *Alignment Panel*	***Draw the following object. Use the picture "Still Life Pumpkins.jpg," and draw an orange box. Use the Align Panel to make sure the rows are lined up.***
6.3 Distribution	This will **Distribute** or space out objects.
Practice Exercise 90 *Distribute* *Anchor Points*	***Window Menu → Align Panel → Distribute Anchor Points.***
6.4 Rotate Tool	This **Rotates** objects and text boxes around a fixed point. This object is called a **Spirograph**.
Student Project V *Spirograph*	1. ***Draw a single Line.*** 2. ***Use the Variable Width Profile*** Uniform ***in the line options → Choose the*** 3. ***Select the Rotate Tool.*** 4. ***Move the center point to the end of the line (on the bottom anchor point).*** 5. ***Hold Alt Key → Move the line to make a copy. (grab the top Anchor Point)*** (**Mac CS6:** *Use the option Key*). 6. ***Repeat the operation by Ctrl D or Object Menu → Transform → Transform again.*** (**Mac CS6:** *Use the **Command D Key**).*

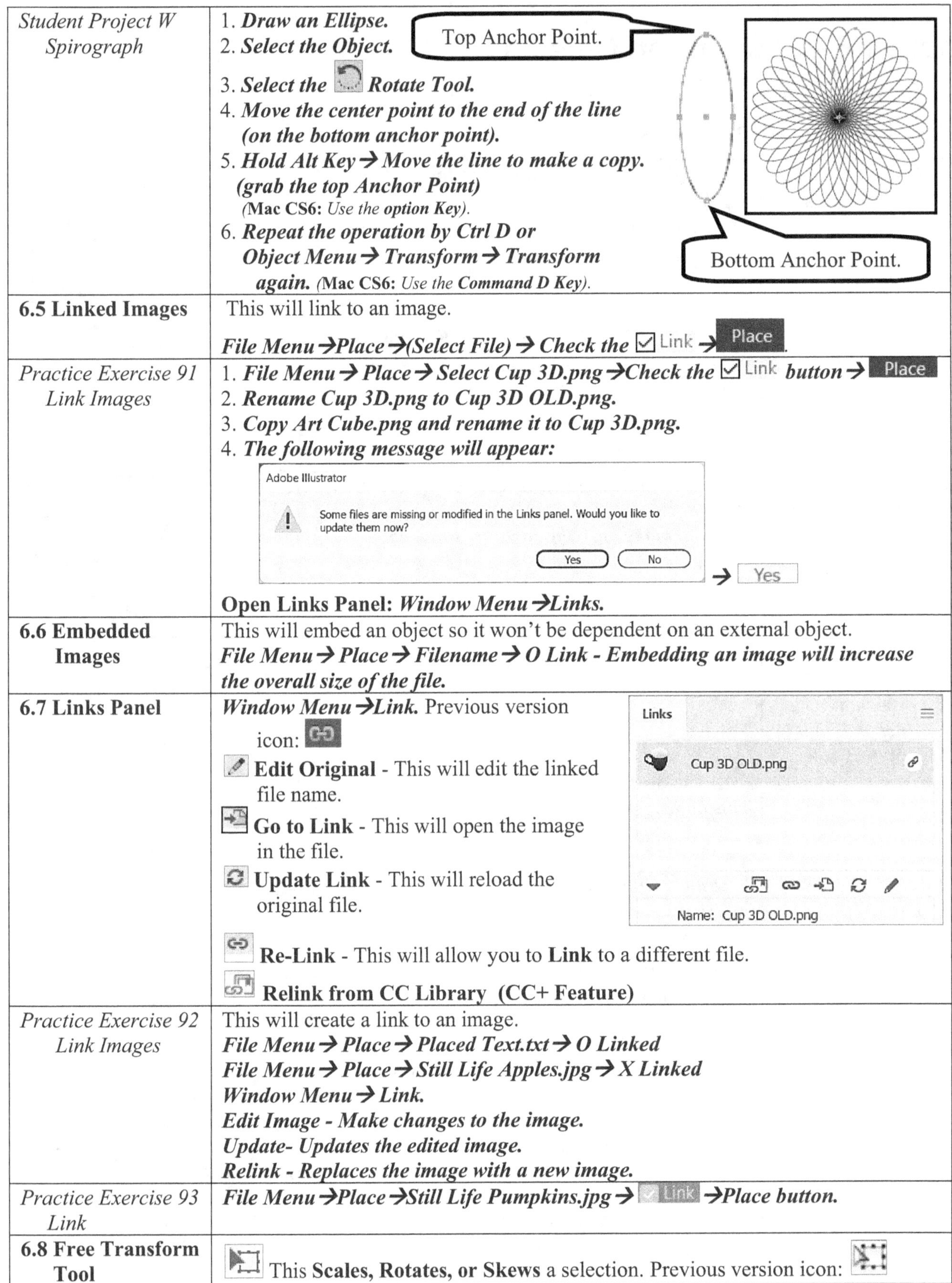

Student Project W Spirograph	1. ***Draw an Ellipse.*** 2. ***Select the Object.*** 3. ***Select the*** Rotate Tool. 4. ***Move the center point to the end of the line (on the bottom anchor point).*** 5. ***Hold Alt Key → Move the line to make a copy. (grab the top Anchor Point)*** (**Mac CS6:** *Use the option Key*). 6. ***Repeat the operation by Ctrl D or Object Menu → Transform → Transform again.*** *(***Mac CS6:*** *Use the ***Command D Key***)*.
6.5 Linked Images	This will link to an image. ***File Menu→Place→(Select File) → Check the*** ☑ Link → Place .
Practice Exercise 91 Link Images	1. ***File Menu → Place → Select Cup 3D.png →Check the*** ☑ Link ***button →*** Place 2. ***Rename Cup 3D.png to Cup 3D OLD.png.*** 3. ***Copy Art Cube.png and rename it to Cup 3D.png.*** 4. ***The following message will appear:*** → Yes **Open Links Panel:** *Window Menu →Links.*
6.6 Embedded Images	This will embed an object so it won't be dependent on an external object. ***File Menu → Place → Filename → O Link - Embedding an image will increase the overall size of the file.***
6.7 Links Panel	*Window Menu →Link.* Previous version icon: **Edit Original** - This will edit the linked file name. **Go to Link** - This will open the image in the file. **Update Link** - This will reload the original file. **Re-Link** - This will allow you to **Link** to a different file. **Relink from CC Library** (**CC+ Feature**)
Practice Exercise 92 Link Images	This will create a link to an image. ***File Menu → Place → Placed Text.txt → O Linked*** ***File Menu → Place → Still Life Apples.jpg → X Linked*** ***Window Menu → Link.*** ***Edit Image - Make changes to the image.*** ***Update- Updates the edited image.*** ***Relink - Replaces the image with a new image.***
Practice Exercise 93 Link	***File Menu →Place →Still Life Pumpkins.jpg →*** Link ***→Place button.***
6.8 Free Transform Tool	This **Scales, Rotates, or Skews** a selection. Previous version icon:

Practice Exercise 94 Free Transform	*Draw a Star→ Select the Free Transform Tool → Scale, rotate or skew the object.*
6.9 Transform Panel Additional CC+ Feature	This includes **Transform Tools, Shear, and Rotate:** *Window Menu→ Transform.*
6.10 Scale Tool	This **Resizes** objects around a fixed point. Previous version icon:
Practice Exercise 95 Scale	*Draw a Rectangle →Select the Rectangle → Scale Tool→Scale the Rectangle by grabbing the endpoint→ Drag outward to scale the rectangle.*
6.11 Shear Tool	This slants or skews an object around a fixed point. Previous version icon: *Draw rectangle→ Shear Tool→Shear the rectangle.*
Student Project X 3D Image	**Design Technique** **These are the steps to be taken to create a 3D object:** 1. *Draw 1 box using the Rectangle Tool: Select the Rectangle Tool→ Hold the Shift Key down → Draw the rectangle. Tip: The Shift Key will create a perfect square box.* 2. Use the **Alt Key** to make 2 copies: *Select the square box→ Hold the Alt key down→ Drag n drop the square box→ Let go of the Alt key.* 3. Size the Rectangles down to ½ the size: *Select the middle handle of the upper square box→ Resize the image.* 4. *Repeat the operation for the side square.* 5. *Select the Top Box using the Select Tool →Select the Rotate the Tool and move the center point to the lower corner.* 6. *Select the Side Box using the Select Tool →Select the Rotate the Tool and move the center point to the lower corner.* 7. *Select Top Box using the Select Tool→ Shear Tool→ Hold the upper right corner and shear the box.* 8. *Select Side Box using the Select Tool → Shear Tool→ Hold the upper right corner and shear the box.* 9. The 3D box will look similar to the following:

Student Project Y *3D Images*	**Use the Rectangle Tool to create 3 boxes, the Shear Tool to create the 3D look, the Selection Tool to move into place, Ellipse Tool to draw the circle image, and rotation to obtain the angle of the circle images.**
Student Project Z *3D Images*	**File Menu → Place → Kids.jpg → Use the Alt Key to copy 3 Images → Use the Shear Tool. You can also try the Transform Panel.** (**Mac CS6:** *Use the* **Option Key** *instead of the* **Alt Key**).
Student Project AA *Shadow*	**Use the Transparency Panel.** **(May need to use Shear, Rotate, and Reflect Tools).**

Student Project BB
Creating Card
	Create a greeting card by folding 8 ½ X 11 paper.
	
	1a. CC: *File→New→Print Tab → Letter Size Paper →* Landscape.
	1b. *CS6: File Menu → New → Letter Size → Landscape:*
	2. *View→Rulers→Show Rulers.*
	3. *View→Guides→Unlock Guides.*
	4. *Edit→Preferences→Units→General: Inches.*
	  (**Mac CS6: Illustrator Menu→Preferences**).
	5. Drag the guides in the middle:
	  Move Guides to *4.25 X 5.5.*
	
	Box 1 - Create a logo drawing your initials using the **Pencil Tool**. Then, adjust the **Brush Definition** to obtain the desired effect. Also, use the **Pen Tool** to create a path and text on a path. **"Jasper series Card collection - Fall Edition"**
	Box 2 - Add the image **Still Life Apples.jpg**
	Box 3 - Use a text box to create the message: **"Thinking of You!! I wanted to send you a warm wish and let you know I am just thinking of you. Love, Jason."** Format the text using the **Font Type: Blackadder ITC.** *Select text box→ Object→ Rasterize →OK →Rotate text box.*
	Box 4 - Leave Blank

Student Project CC *3D Text*	***File Menu → Place →*** ***Art Cube.png → Text Tool → Draw text*** ***box → Select text box →*** ***Use a combination of the Selections Tool*** ***to move the text and the Shear Tool to*** ***shear the text box.***	

Section 2 - Optional Topics

6.12 Puppet Warp Tool CC+	This will allow you to twist and distort parts of your artwork, such that the transformations appear natural. You can add, move, and rotate pins to seamlessly transform your artwork into different variations using this tool.
Practice Exercise 96 Selection	1, Draw a Rectangle: ***Rectangle Tool → Draw Rectangle***. 2. Select Object: ***Selection Tool → Select Rectangle***. 3. Select the Puppet Warp Tool: ***Puppet Warp Tool***. 4. Pin Parts of the object: ***Click on the Rectangle***. 5. ***Move the Pin to Warp the Rectangle***.
6.13 Reflect Tool	This **Flips** objects over a fixed axis. Previous version icon:
Practice Exercise 97 Reflect Tool	***Select object → Reflection Tool → Click reflection point (under object) → Reflect object***.
6.14 Reshape Tool	This **Adjusts** selected anchor points while keeping the overall detail of the path intact. Previous version icon:
Practice Exercise 98 Reshape Tool	***Use the Pencil to draw a curved line → Reshape Tool → reshape the line***.
6.15 Width Tool (Shift W)	This allows you to create a stroke with a variable **Width**. Previous version icon:
Practice Exercise 99 Width Tool	***Draw a rectangle → Select the Width Tool → Stretch the width of the line around the rectangle***.

6.16 Warp Tool (Shift R)	This mold objects with the movement of the cursor (like molding clay). Previous version icon:	
Practice Exercise 100 Warp Tool	***Draw a Star→ Select the Warp Tool→ Warp the object.***	
6.17 Twirl Tool	This creates swirling distortions within an object. Previous version icon:	
Practice Exercise 101 Twirl Tool	***Draw a Star → Select the Twirl Tool→ Twirl the object.***	
6.18 Pucker Tool	This deflates an object by moving control points toward the cursor. Previous version icon:	
Practice Exercise 102 Pucker Tool	***Draw a Star → Select the Pucker Tool→ Pucker the object.***	
6.19 Bloat Tool	This inflates an object by moving control points away from the cursor. Previous version icon:	
Practice Exercise 103 Bloat Tool	***Draw a Star→ Select the Bloat Tool → Bloat the object.***	
6.20 Scallop Tool	This adds random curved details to the outline of an object. Previous version icon:	
Practice Exercise 104 Scallop Tool	***Draw a Star→ Select the Scallop Tool→ Scallop the object.***	
6.21 Crystallize Tool	This adds random spiked details to the outline of an object. Previous version icon:	
Practice Exercise 105 Crystallize Tool	***Draw a Star→ Select the Crystallize Tool→ Crystallize the object.***	
6.22 Wrinkle Tool	This adds wrinkle-like details to the outline of an object. Previous version icon:	
Practice Exercise 106 Wrinkle Tool	***Draw a Star→ Select the Wrinkle Tool → Wrinkle the object.***	

Chapter 7 - Customizing Artwork

We will now use our new skills to develop and create some artwork.

Section 1 - Core Topics

Concept	Explanation / *Command String in italic*
7.1 Arrow Heads	This adds **Arrow Heads**. 1. *Line Tool→Draw a Line→ Select the Line.* 2a. *Window Menu → Stroke → Show Options.* **Tip:** The Show Options is located in the Upper right corner. 2b. *Line Tool→Draw a Line→ Select the Line →Line Tool Options→Stroke.* 3. Arrowheads:
7.2 Fill Tools	This includes **Fill, Swatches Panel, Brushes, Opacit**y, and the **Eyedropper Tool**.
7.3 Brushes Panel	This contains additional **Brush Styles**. The lower left corner icon contains additional symbols. *Window Menu→ Brushes Panel→ Click on the Icon.* CS5 Icon: CS6+
7.4 Graphic Style Panel	This contains additional graphics objects. The lower left corner icon contains additional Graphic Styles. *Window Menu→ Graphic Styles Panel→Click on the Icon.* CS5 Icon:
Practice Exercise 107 Artistic Effects	*File Menu→ Open→ Rock Climb.ai.* *Window Menu→ Graphic Styles Panel→ Use: Artistic Effects or 3D Effects.*
7.5 Swatch Panel	This contains additional swatches. The lower left corner icon contains additional swatches. *Window Menu→ Swatch Panel→ Click on the Icon.* CS5 Icon:
7.6 Symbol Library	This will add **Library** shapes to the **Artboard** and can add the shape to the **Symbols Library**. The lower left corner icon contains additional **Symbols**. You can drag & drop from each **Library** or add to the main **Library**. Click on the Icon. **CS5** Icon: *Window Menu→Symbols→ Symbols Library Menu→Choose a Library: Tiki*
7.7 Gradient Tool	The **Gradient Tool** will allow you to create **Gradients** in Black, White, and **Color**.
7.8 Gradient Style	This applies effects such as **Transparency, Fill, Stroke**, etc.
7.9 Gradient Panel	To create a color **Gradient**, you need to change the stop box on the **Gradient** slider. *Window Menu→ Gradient Panel.* **Tip:** When you click the stop box, choose the More Icon to change to CMYK color mode. Previous version icon:
Practice Exercise 108 Gradient	*Create the following:*

Section 2 - Optional Topics

7.10 Appearance Panel	You can change opacity, stroke, fill, and effects. They can be turned on/off to view results. This is done by turning on/off the eye. Add multiple strokes to a text image and move the order etc. ***Window Menu→Appearance.*** Previous version icon:
Practice Exercise 109 Appearance Panel	***Appearance Panel*** ***File Menu→Open→Rock Climb.ai*** ***Window Menu→Appearance Panel*** ***Select image→Apply a warp wave effect Fx→ Warp→ Wave*** 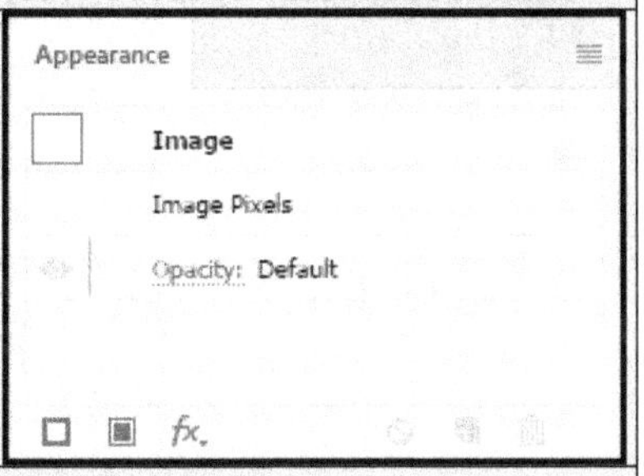
7.11 Patterns	This creates **Patterns** that can be used to duplicate a small area throughout the object used.
Practice Exercise 110 Pattern	1. Create a small **Pattern** in **Photoshop** in jpg format: ***File Menu→ Open→Pattern1.jpg.*** 2. Select **Pattern:** ***Selection Tool → Select a pattern.***  3. Make **Pattern:** ***Object Menu→ Pattern→Make.*** 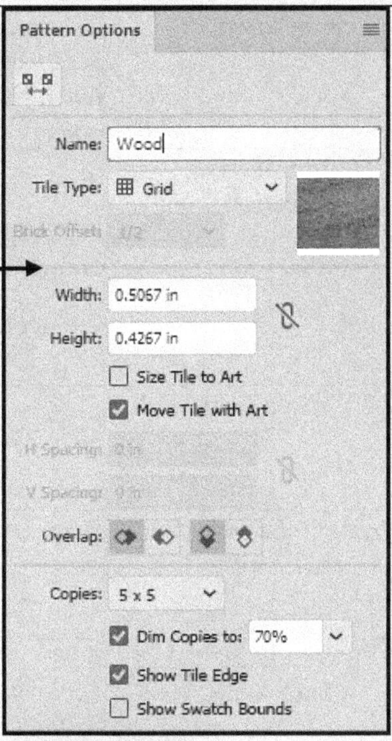 4. Notice the **Pattern** will be located in the **Swatches Panel**. If the new **Pattern** is not visible: ***Show Swatch Kinds Menu→***   Show Pattern Swatches Swatches — Show 5. Draw the Pattern: ***Rectangle Tool→ Set the options to fill the Background with the new pattern.***  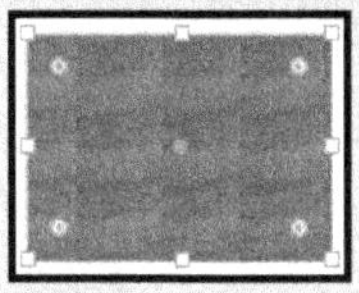 Rectangle — Stroke: 6. Draw a rectangle.
7.12 Shape Builder Tool	This merges simple shapes to create custom, complex shapes. CS5 Icon: 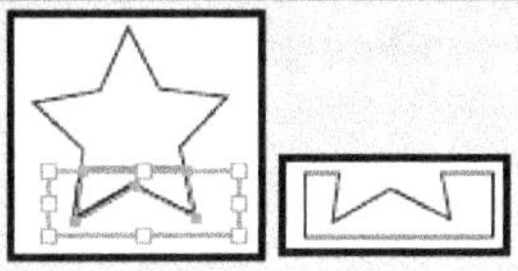
Practice Exercise 111 Shape Builder Tool	***Draw and overlap a star and a triangle→ Select both objects → Shape Builder Tool→ Click the rectangle→ Move the objects apart.***

7.13 Live Paint Bucket	This paints the faces and edges of **Live Paint** groups with the current paint attributes. Previous version icon:
7.14 Live Paint Selection Tool	This selects faces and edges within **Live Paint** groups. **(Shift L)** CS5 Icon:
7.15 Perspective Grid Tool	This allows for creating and rendering artwork in **Perspective**. CS5 Icon: **To turn Off:** *Ctrl Shift I*
Practice Exercise 112 Perspective	*Add a Perspective grid to the artwork → Add objects (rectangle, oval, etc) and they will take on the perspective.* *Once you add the perspective grid to the Artboard → All objects added will follow the perspective.*
7.16 Perspective Selection Tool	This allows you to bring objects, text, and symbols in **Perspective**, as well as move objects in **Perspective** or move objects to be perpendicular to each other. Cs5 Icon:
7.17 Mesh Tool	This creates and edits meshes and mesh envelopes. CS5 Icon:
Practice Exercise 113 Mesh Tool	*Draw a star → Select the Mesh Tool → Click several times in the star → Move one of the points out of the star.*
7.18 Gradient Tool	This grades color from light to dark. It creates a gradient with 2 or more stop points. CS5 Icon:
Practice Exercise 114 Gradient Tool	*Pencil Tool → Draw enclosed area → Gradient Panel → Click on Reverse Gradient Button → Use gradient Tool to set gradient range.*
7.19 Eyedropper Tool	The **Eyedropper Tool** (I) samples and applies color, type, and appearance attributes, including effects, from objects. Previous version icon:
Practice Exercise 115 Eyedropper Tool	*Select the Eyedropper Tool → Click on any color image → The default color will be defined.*

7.20 Blend Tool	This creates a series of objects **Blended** between the color and shape of multiple objects. Previous version icon:
Practice Exercise 116 Blend Tool	***Draw 2 objects, select both images, select Blend Tool, then draw across both objects.***
7.21 Symbol Spray Tool	This duplicates the **Symbol** by spraying. Previous version icon:
Practice Exercise 117 Spray Tool	***A****dd a symbol from the symbol Pane* ♣ *→ Select the Symbol Spray Tool→ Spray the Artboard.*
7.22 Symbol Shifter Tool	This moves **Symbol** instances and changes the stacking order. Previous version icon:
Practice Exercise 118 Symbol Shifter	***Use the Symbol Shifter.***
7.23 Symbol Scruncher Tool	This moves **Symbol** instances closer together or farther apart. Previous version icon:
Practice Exercise 119 Scruncher Tool	***Use the Scruncher Tool.***
7.24 Symbol Sizer Tool	This resizes **Symbol** instances. Previous version icon:
Practice Exercise 120 Symbol Spray	***Use the Symbol Sizer Tool.***
7.25 Symbol Spinner Tool	This rotates **Symbol** instances. Previous version icon:
Practice Exercise 121 Symbol Spinner	***Use the Symbol Spinner Tool.***
7.26 Symbol Stainer Tool	This colorizes **Symbol** instances. Previous version icon:
Practice Exercise 122 Symbol Stainer	***Use the Symbol Stainer Tool.***
7.27 Symbol Screener Tool	This applies opacity to **Symbol** instances. Previous version icon:
Practice Exercise 123 Symbol Screener	***Use the Symbol Screener Tool.***
7.28 Symbol Styler Tool	This applies the selected style to **Symbol** instances. Previous version icon:
Practice Exercise 124 Symbol Styler	***Use the Symbol Styler Tool.***

7.29 Slice Tool	This **Slices** a graphics object into two pieces. It divides artwork into separate web images. Previous version icon:	
Practice Exercise 125 Slice Tool	A*dd a symbol➔ Select the Slice Tool➔ Slice the symbol.*	
7.30 Slice Selection (Shift K)	This **Slices** a selected object. Selects web slices. Previous version icon:	
Practice Exercise 126 Slice Selection	*Select the middle section.*	
7.31 Column Graph Tool	This creates **Graphs** that compare values using vertical **Columns**. Previous version icon:	
7.32 Stacked Column Graph Tool	This creates **Graphs** that are similar to column **Graphs**, but stacks the columns on top of one another, instead of side by side. This **Graph** type is useful for showing the relationship of parts to the total. Previous version icon:	
7.33 Bar Graph Tool	This creates **Graphs** that are similar to column **Graphs** but positions the bars horizontally instead of vertically. Previous version icon:	
7.34 Stacked Bar Graph Tool	This creates **Graphs** that are similar to stacked column **Graphs** but stacks the bars horizontally instead of vertically. Previous version icon:	
7.35 Line Graph Tool	This creates **Graphs** that use points to represent one or more sets of values with a different **Line** joining the points in each set. This type of **Graph** is often used to show the trend of one or more subjects over a period of time. Previous version icon:	
7.36 Area Graph Tool	This creates **Graphs** that are similar to line **Graphs**, but emphasize totals as well as changes in values. Previous version icon:	
7.37 Scatter Graph Tool	This creates **Graphs** that plot data points as paired sets of coordinates along the x and y-axes. **Scatter Graphs** are useful for identifying patterns or trends in data. They also can indicate whether variables affect one another. Previous version icon:	
7.38 Pie Graph Tool	This creates circular **Graphs** whose wedges represent the relative percentages of the values compared. Previous version icon:	
7.39 Radar Graph Tool	This creates **Graphs** that compare sets of values at given points in time or in particular categories and are displayed in a circular format. This type of **Graph** is also called a web **Graph**. Previous version icon:	

Chapter 8 - Begin Deployment

When you are finished with your artwork, you will need to save it in various formats for permanent storage.

Section 1 - Core Topics

Concept	Explanation / *Command String in italic*
8.1 Find and Replace	This will **Find** text and **Replace** it.
Practice Exercise 127 Find/Replace	***Edit Menu →Find and Replace.***
8.2 Spell Checking	**Spell Checks** the selected words.
Practice Exercise 128 Spell Checking	***Edit Menu → Spell Checking.***
8.3 Custom Dictionaries	This will allow you to add **Custom** words to the **Dictionary**.
Practice Exercise 129 Custom Dictionary	***Edit Menu → Edit Custom Dictionary.***
8.4 Wrap Text	This will **Wrap Text** around images.
Practice Exercise 130 Wrap	***Add a text box with text →add a symbol from the symbol library → Select Symbol, Object Menu → Text Wrap → Make,*** ***Object Menu → Text Wrap → Text Wrap Options.***
8.5 Exporting	This will allow you to **Export** a single **Artboard** to a graphics file. If you have multiple **Artboards** defined the default options will export both **Artboards** to a single file. **Tip: Export selected objects:** *Select all objects →r-click on object →Export selection.*
Practice Exercise 131 Save For Web	***File Menu →Export.*** *Also try:* ***File →Save as and File →Save for web*** *and devices.*
Student Project DD Wrap	1. ***File Menu →Place → 3D Cup File Menu → Place → Give My Regards to Broadway.txt.*** 2. ***Select 3D Cup → Object Menu → Arrange → Bring to Front*** Give my regards to Broadway, Remember me to Herald Square. Tell all the gang at Forty Second Street That I will soon be there. Whisper of how I'm yearning To mingle with the old time throng. Give my regards to old Broadway And say that I'll be there ere long. ***Select 3D Cup → Object Menu → Wrap Text →Make.***
8.6 Export Multiple Artboards	If you have **Multiple Artboards** containing designs, you can save each **Artboard** to a different file. ***File menu →Export →Export as →*** ☑ Use Artboards This will save each **Artboard** as a different file name such as: ***Artboard-01.jpg and Artboard-02.jpg*** File name: Artboard Save as type: JPEG (*.JPG) ☑ Use Artboards ◉ All ○ Range:

8.7 Export **Asset** **Or Artboard**	**Method 1, 2, and 3** below will take you to the same interface to **Export** a selected object or objects to a **PNG** or **JPG** file format. When you select an object choose **Assets** and to **Export** the **Artboard** choose **Artboard** below. **Tip:** This feature is supported in **Illustrator CC** and is very similar to older versions.

Practice Exercise 132
Methods 1,2,3
 	
Illustrator CC
	Method 1 - Open desired Artboard →Select Image →Right-click on the Image →
	    Export Selection →Asset or Artboard.
	Method 2 - Open desired Artboard →Select Image →File Menu →
	    Export Selection →Asset or Artboard.
	Method 3 - File Menu →Export →Export for Screens → →Asset or Artboard.
	1. **Asset vs Artboard tab**
	
	2. **Export To -** Specify the folder.
	
	3. **Open Location after Export**
	4. **Create Sub-Folders**
	
	5. **Format>**
	
	6. ⚙ **Gear Settings -** Set the background to **Transparent, White,** or **Black.**
	Interlaced - Displays partial image on the web which allows someone to decide to abort sooner. Non-Laced will load 10% faster.
	Anti-aliasing - Smooths the edges.
	PNG - Portable Network Graphics.
	PNG-8 - 256 colors similar to GIF. Usually a smaller file size.
	PNG-24 - True color, high resolution, large file size.

Practice Exercise 133 *Method 4*	**Method 4 - Save For Web:** *File Menu →Export →Save for Web (Legacy) →* *Save for Web interface →GIF, JPG, PNG8, PNG24.*

Practice Exercise 134
Method 5
	Method 5 - Export As: This will export all Artboards.
	    File Menu →Export →Export As →(Filename) →
	    Background Color=Transparent.

Section 2 - Optional Topics

8.8 Optimize Content for the Web	CS6: *File Menu → Save for Web* CC: *File Menu → Export → Save for Web*
8.9 Optimize Content For PDF Documents	*File Menu → Save as → Save as type: Adobe PDF(.PDF)*
8.10 Create Image Using Artboard	*Object Menu → Artboard → Fit to Artboard Boundaries.*
8.11 Print Tiling Tool	This adjusts the page grid to control where artwork appears on the printed page. It is located under the **Hand Tool**.
Practice Exercise 135 Print Tilting Tool	*Zoom out → Print Tilting Tool → Adjust the printed page outline using the Print Tilting Tool.*
8.12 File Formats	This are a list of file formats that can be used with **Illustrator**: **Photoshop(.PSD) -** This saves and supports all **Photoshop** features. It does not lose quality or collapse layers when saved. However, it is not suitable for the Web. **PNG - Portable Network Graphics (Png)**. This is a cross between **Gif** and **Jpeg**. It supports up to 48-bit RGB color and 16-bit grayscale. It also supports transparent images. However, you may lose some quality depending on the **Save** options. **JPEG - Joint Photographic Experts Group (Jpeg or Jpg)**. This is used for photos and contains millions of colors. It does not support transparent images or the 8-bit color spectrum. However, you may lose some quality depending on the **Save** options. When saving to a **Jpeg** file, it will ask for the quality of 10 to be used for on-screen viewing and 12 is maximized for quality printing. **CompuServe GIF - Graphics Interchange Format (GIF)** is a small file size. It contains only 256 colors and supports transparent images. However, you may lose some quality depending on the **Save** options. If an image has a limited number of solid colors, **Gif** will be an acceptable solution. **Photoshop PDF -** Portable Document Format (**PDF**). *File Menu →Save As →Photoshop PDF →High Quality, Press Quality, and Smallest File Size.* **Photoshop EPS -** This is an **Encapsulated PostScript** (**EPS**) language. It is **Adobe's PostScript** printing format and preserves all raster and vector images. However, data is rasterized when opened in **Photoshop** and **EPS** does not support **Layers.** **Photoshop RAW -** This is a high-resolution file format usually taken by a high-powered camera, and saved in a Photoshop **RAW** format type. However, it does not preserve the original native camera **RAW** format. **BMP - Bit Map** image or a **Raster** image is a very large file size. The **Windows Paint** program will save to the **bmp** file type by default. **TIFF - Tagged-Image File Format (TIFF, TIF)** is a bit map image format and supports layers. This allows file compression because the file size is very large. It is often used for scanners and fax machines. **Large Document (PSB) -** The **Large Document Format (PSB)** supports documents up to 300,000 pixels in any dimension. It supports layers, effects,

and filters.

Dicom - The **DICOM (Digital Imaging and Communications in Medicine)** format is commonly used for the transfer and storage of medical images, such as ultrasounds and scans.

Photoshop DCS - The **Desktop Color Separations (DCS)** format is a version of the standard **EPS** format that allows you to save color separations of **CMYK** images. You can also use the **DCS 2.0** format to export images containing spot channels. To print **DCS** files, you must use a **PostScript** printer.

IFF Format - IFF (Interchange File Format) is a general-purpose data storage format that can associate and store multiple types of data. **IFF** is portable and has extensions that support still-picture, sound, music, video, and textual data.

JPEG 2000 - The **JPEG 2000** offers advantages such as support for higher bit depths, more advanced compressions, and a lossless compression option.

PCX - The **PCX** format is commonly used by **IBM PC-compatible** computers. Most PC software supports version 5 of PCX format.

Pixar - The **Pixar** format is designed specifically for high-end graphics applications such as those used for rendering three-dimensional images and animation.

Portable Bit Map - The **Portable Bit Map (PBM)** file format, also known as Portable **Bitmap Library** and **Portable Binary Map**, supports monochrome bitmaps (one bit per pixel).

Scitex - The **Scitex Continuous Tone (CT)** format is used for high-end image processing on **Scitex** computers.

Targa - The **Targa (TGA)** format is designed for systems using the **Truevision** video board and is commonly supported by **MS-DOS** color applications.

Chapter 9 - Advanced Topics

There are also some additional, advanced topics you may find to be useful.

Concept	Explanation / *Command String in italic*
9.1 Layers	*Window Menu→Layers.* This selects the drop-down arrow to view the objects in the **Layer**. Turn off the **Layer** and select the eye. The selected **Layers** are the active **Layers** where objects are placed.
9.2 Library	This allows you to add a symbol to the Library. You can access many stock photos by choosing the **Adobe Stock** option.
Practice Exercise 136 Libraries	*Window Menu → Libraries → ⌄ →* Adobe Stock →Search Feather feather
9.3 Pathfinder	This will allow you to combine vector objects to create a variety of shapes. **Compound shapes** will allow you to add, subtract, intersect, and exclude. **Pathfinder effects** let you combine multiple objects using interaction modes. When you use Pathfinder effects, you can't edit the interactions between objects.
Practice Exercise 137 Pathfinder	*Window Menu → Pathfinder.*
9.4 Perspectives	**Perspective Grid Tool**. **Tip:** Click the X to close the perspective. If it doesn't close click on the *Hand Tool, Perspective Grid Tool, then X.*
9.5 Compound Paths	This allows you to cut a hole in an object where it overlaps.

Practice Exercise 138 Compound Path	***Object Menu*** → ***Compound Path*** → ***Make/Release.***
9.6 Trace Artworks	This will allow you to import and **Trace** an imported image.
Practice Exercise 139 Image Trace	***File Menu*** → ***Place*** → ***Gutar.jpg*** → ***Select object*** → ***Window Menu*** →***Image Trace*** → ***View: Outline. New in CS6.***

Index - Graphic Design & Custom Illustrations

Adobe Courseware

Step-By-Step Training Guides and Workbooks

Available on Amazon.com (Search for author, Jeff Hutchinson)

To review a sample book, see the sample video clip, and Amazon reviews, and to purchase: Go To: https://www.elearnlogic.com. These **Step-By-Step Training Guides** focus on specific learning concepts including brief descriptions as well as many short 2-5 minute exercises for practice. The Table of Contents

and Index will allow students to look up desired concepts quickly and easily. These guides are invaluable resources used to build and maintain computer skills for industry, as well as for personal use.

Available in Paperback: $9.95 or Kindle eBook: $5.95

https://www.amazon.com /dp/B0BRQ4NDC6

https://www.amazon.com /dp/B0BRLRSXC8

https://www.amazon.com /dp/1976466695

https://www.amazon.com /dp/1976467004

About the Author

Jeff Hutchinson is a corporate computer trainer and consultant. He teaches **Microsoft** and **Adobe** products from beginning to advanced topics. Jeff has a BS degree from BYU in Computer-Aided

Engineering and owned a computer training and consulting firm in San Francisco, California for several years. He currently works as an independent

https://www.amazon.com/dp/1987724038

computer instructor and these training guides are based on topics most commonly taught.

Contact Information: Jeff Hutchinson, jeffhutch@elearnlogic.com or (801) 376-6687.

Evaluation copy: http://www.elearnlogic.com/

www.ingramcontent.com/pod-product-compliance
Lightning Source LLC
Chambersburg PA
CBHW081534250726
48659CB00009B/2993